The Shadow Cabinet in British Politics

LIBRARY OF POLITICAL STUDIES

GENERAL EDITOR:
PROFESSOR H. VICTOR WISEMAN

Department of Government
University of Exeter

The Shadow Cabinet in British Politics

by D. R. Turner

*Assistant Lecturer in British Government
in the University of Wales
Institute of Science and Technology
Cardiff*

LONDON

ROUTLEDGE & KEGAN PAUL

NEW YORK: HUMANITIES PRESS

First published 1969
by Routledge & Kegan Paul Ltd
Broadway House, 68-74 Carter Lane
London, E.C.4

Printed in Great Britain
by Northumberland Press Limited
Gateshead

SBN 7100 6489 6

General editor's introduction

This series of monographs is designed primarily to meet the needs of students of government, politics, or political science in Universities and other institutions providing courses leading to degrees. Each volume aims to provide a brief general introduction indicating the significance of its topic, e.g. executives, parties, pressure groups, etc., and then a longer 'case study' relevant to the general topic. First year students will thus be introduced to the kind of detailed work on which all generalizations must be based, while more mature students will have an opportunity to become acquainted with recent original research in a variety of fields. The series will eventually provide a comprehensive coverage of most aspects of political science in a more interesting and fundamental manner than in the large volume which often fails to compensate by breadth what it inevitably lacks in depth.

The Shadow Cabinet both derives from and influences the basic features of the British system of government, a two-party system, a desire on the part of voters directly to choose between rival teams of potential Ministers, a belief in constructive opposition by 'Her Majesty's Alternative Government'. Yet very little has been written on this peculiarly British phenomenon, though brief reference is made to it in another volume in this series, *The Tactics of Resignation.* Mr Turner's monograph should therefore be widely welcomed. Within limited space he has traced the history of the idea of a Shadow Cabinet from the third quarter of the nineteenth century to the middle of the twentieth century. He then analyses the working of the 'modern shadow cabinet', bringing out clearly the differences in organization and role between the two major parties. If Sir Ivor Jennings is correct in asserting that the true test of democracy is to ask where the Opposition is, then one test of an effective democracy may be to ask how the Opposition works. This volume provides an important part of the answer to this question.

H.V.W.

Contents

Introduction   page xiii

1   Origins of the idea   1

    The growth of 'organized opposition'   2
    Quasi-cabinets   5
    The 'Cabinet of the Opposition'   9

2   Shadow Cabinets emerge   11

    Opposition still in disarray   11
    The leadership issue   13
    Sir William Harcourt and the Shadow Cabinet   17

3   A steady development   19

    Opposition led in the Commons by Northcote   20
    Gladstone and the Shadow Cabinet   21
    The Liberals in trouble: Chamberlain departs   22
    John Morley and the Shadow Cabinet   24
    *Opposition responsibilities and Ministerial
      appointments*   25
    *Campbell-Bannerman becomes Leader of the
      Opposition*   27
    Balfour and the Conservative Party   28
    The Conservatives and the 1911 Crisis   30
    Further developments up to 1918   32

4 Elected front bench   35

   Emergence of a Labour Opposition in 1922   35
   Relations between the P.L.P and the I.L.P.   40
   Lloyd George and the Liberal Shadow Cabinet   41
   *Amery, Churchill and the Conservative Shadow
     Cabinet*   43

5 From MacDonald to Churchill   46

   Lansbury becomes Leader   47
   An elected Shadow Cabinet and Front Bench   48
   *The Labour Opposition and the Second World
     War*   50
   Victory yet defeat   51
   Churchill as Leader of the Opposition   51
   Opposition becomes more effective   53
   Approach of the 1950 General Election   56

6 The Modern Shadow Cabinet   58

   Divided we fall   59
   Bevan, Greenwood and Crossman   60
   Checks and balances   62
   Extensive network of Committees   65

7 Election and selection   69

   Lord Morrison deplores increasing formalization   71
   P.L.P. Opposition Front Bench 1951-64   72
   Opposition 'double banking'   75
   Approach of the 1964 General Election   77
   'Shadows' into realities   80

8 Conservatives in Opposition   84

   Sir Alec Douglas-Home's Shadow Cabinet   85
   Re-allocation of responsibilities   87
   Edward Heath becomes Leader   91
   Heath's 'Shadow Government'   93
   *The Conservatives and the 1966 General
      Election*   95

   Bibliography   97

   Suggestions for Further Reading   101

   Note on Sources   105

The longer and more varied the politicians' experience of parliament and of office, the more skilled they will be in employing the techniques of government and opposition— techniques which no one else can really appreciate unless he has been trained in the use of them. This is the main reason, I think, why we need a change of government now and then. It is desirable that the men who have been criticizing should be put in a position where they have to take responsibility, and that no government should grow to think that it is ordained by God and settled for life. The rationale of our parliamentary system is that the Opposition is an alternative Government. This means that all front bench politicians must be masters of both sorts of techniques, those of making the government machine work and those of criticizing its performance. I do not think that we can do without these techniques in any sort of state that I should care to live in.

PROFESSOR J. D. B. MILLER

An extract from Politicians, *an inaugural lecture at the University, Leicester, 25 February 1958*

Introduction

This study will attempt to trace and examine the history, growth and development of the body popularly known as the 'Shadow Cabinet' in British politics.

The Shadow Cabinet is concerned with power and aspirations of power. The personnel of Shadow Cabinets are, or at least should be, constantly prepared to assume the mantle of government. It is therefore surprising to discover that the Shadow Cabinet is a subject upon which there is remarkably little published material. This appears to be the first attempt to write a book specifically about this body, what few references there are being scattered through most of the standard works on British Government.

One point which should be stressed at the very outset is the existence of an officially recognized Opposition and Leader of the Opposition, a fact often overlooked, which, together with the two party system, is considered to be an outstanding feature of the British Constitution.

Of course, there have been, there are and undoubtedly there will always be other political parties, but the two-party system as it works in Britain means that there are only two teams capable of forming independent administrations. The system thus lends itself admirably to the operation of a Government and an Opposition and to this fact both the Cabinet and the Shadow Cabinet owe their existence. To quote the late Sir Ivor Jennings, 'the Opposition is at once the alternative to the Government and a focus for the discontent of the people'.

What, in fact, is a Shadow Cabinet? Sir Ivor Jennings called it an 'imitation, by no means too pale, of the Cabinet', which is that select group of senior Ministers drawn from both Houses of Parliament, presided over by the Prime Minister, which constitutes the central co-ordinating and driving force of the Government. In so far as the term 'Shadow Cabinet' implies a form or modification of the Cabinet, it is safe to assume that the Shadow Cabinet is a post-Cabinet development. As Opposition became more formally organized from the mid-nineteenth century onwards, a specific group of Opposition leaders emerged to direct and co-ordinate the actions of the Opposition. Since these men were usually ex-Ministers, their meetings came to be known as meetings of the 'ex-Cabinet' or 'late Cabinet'. They were, in fact, a Cabinet of the Opposition, or a Shadow Cabinet.

It does not seem possible to give a specific date for the emergence of the Shadow Cabinet, the idea gradually emerging over a number of years to be accepted as just one more convention in Britain's 'unwritten' Constitution. As will be seen, various writers have attempted to give dates for the birth of the Shadow Cabinet, though none can be accepted with any degree of certainty. What has been described as the 'old practice' of holding Shadow Cabinets has continued and 'undergone changes of emphasis which reflect the developments in government' (Mackintosh, 1962, 447).

The most valid reason for the continued existence, and indeed expansion, of the Shadow Cabinet lies in its providing a recognizable and acceptable alternative team from which a prospective Prime Minister can select his senior colleagues. It is important that this team has recognized leaders. In this way, the elector is able to decide which team is more likely to represent his or her wishes in Parliament. The validity of this statement is borne out by the Shadow Cabinet team announced by Mr Edward Heath following the defeat of the Conservatives in the 1966 General Election. It is a young team, quite small in number, chosen with the 1970s in mind. Those older members unlikely to be available for possible office following a full five year term of Labour government have largely returned to the back-benches or been allocated to other party responsibilities.

Prior to examining the composition of the Shadow

Cabinet, reference should be made to certain problems which exist in regard to terminology. The expression 'Shadow Cabinet' is a popular one, though it is now being used with increasing regularity by the political parties, the press and political commentators. Technically, the Conservative Party uses the term 'Consultative Committee' and the Labour Party, 'Parliamentary Committee'.

The Labour Party has had a Parliamentary Committee since 1923, consisting of twelve Members of Parliament elected at the opening of every session of Parliament in November by those members of the Parliamentary Party (P.L.P.) in Opposition with seats in the House of Commons. In addition to the elected members, there are six *ex officio* members, namely the Leader and Deputy Leader of the Party, the Chief Whip in the House of Commons, the Leader of the Labour Peers, the Peers' Chief Whip and their elected representative, giving a total Labour Shadow Cabinet membership of eighteen persons. However, a Labour Party Leader in Opposition does now allocate responsibility on the Opposition Front Bench to other persons than those elected and *ex officio* members of the Parliamentary Committee, swelling the ranks of the Opposition Front Bench during 1964 to something like forty persons.

On the other hand, the leader of the Conservative Party in Opposition, though now himself elected by the Party in Parliament, is free to choose his own Shadow Cabinet colleagues. Similarly, however, the Conservative Leader allocates responsibility to senior and junior Front Bench spokesmen, so that Sir Alec Douglas-Home's Shadow Cabinet in February 1965 numbered twenty-one persons with thirty-six Front Bench spokesmen and ten whips. An equivalent list issued by Mr Edward Heath in October 1965 contained seventy-two names, truly a 'Shadow Government' (*The Times*, 6 October 1965). The year 1966 was to witness a dramatic reversal of this trend towards a complete Shadow Government team, the Front Bench announced by Mr Heath following the 1966 Election defeat totalling twenty-seven spokesmen.

Undoubtedly, one of the focal issues to be examined will be the difference between formally and informally elected Opposition Front Benches, the Labour Party combining both the elective and selective principles, whilst the Conservative and Liberal Parties have retained the selection by Leader process. The question of how influential are the members of Shadow Cabinets and to what extent any principal of collective responsibility operates in Opposition will also be examined, as will the relationship between Opposition responsibilities and ministerial appointments. Whilst there are not many examples of Opposition and, more particularly, Shadow Cabinet resignations, those which are on record—such as Churchill and Amery in the 1930s, Bevan in the 1950s and, amongst the Front Benchers, Crossman and Maude—provide a fascinating insight into the machinery of Opposition and the Shadow Cabinet. Even more recently there has been the case of Enoch Powell, first asked by his Leader for a promise of good conduct to ensure his future inclusion in the Shadow Cabinet and then dismissed some two years later following a speech upon race relations in Wolverhampton.

Membership of Shadow Cabinets has never constituted a right to inclusion in any subsequent Government, just as ex-Ministers need not be included in Shadow Cabinets, though it is remarkable to note how close the relationship is between the two. In the majority of cases, the 'shadows' do, in fact, become, what may be termed, 'realities'.

1
Origins of the idea

The expression, 'His Majesty's Opposition' . . . embodies
the greatest contribution of the nineteenth century to the
art of government, that of a party out of power which is
recognized as perfectly loyal to the institutions of the state
and ready to come into office without a shock to the
political traditions of the nation.

A. L. Lowell, *Government of England*

How long has Britain possessed a Shadow Cabinet? By the
second half of the nineteenth century, a 'Loyal Opposition'
had become a recognized and established part of Britain's
unwritten Constitution. Informal meetings of small groups
of ex-Cabinet Ministers were quite common. Whether or
not such gatherings can be regarded as early examples of
Opposition Shadow Cabinets is open to question. However,
it is abundantly clear that it was through meetings such as
these that the seeds of the modern Shadow Cabinet 'system'
were sown.

The development of, what may be termed, 'organized
Opposition' has followed no clear pattern, depending rather
more upon the effectiveness of the Ministry in office and the
attitudes of those in Opposition at any given period in
history. A number of attempts have been made to establish
the earliest recorded examples of organized parliamentary
Opposition and, indeed, the Shadow Cabinet. Each and
every one of these estimations can, and must, be questioned. For example, the year 1836 saw Sir Robert Peel
leading the Opposition against Melbourne and his colleagues. Faced with elements of discord in the Tory ranks,
Peel apparently called a meeting of some prominent members of his former, very short-lived, Cabinet. Peel has been
described as thereby making 'a precedent of importance'

by thus summoning members of his late Cabinet (Keith, 1952, i, 1457). Whilst undoubtedly an early example of organized opposition consultation, it is far more doubtful whether any precedent was established, indeed highly unlikely. This is not to deny that such examples are valuable to the historian and student of British Government. Gradually light is being thrown upon this vast and fascinating subject. Nevertheless, echoing the words of Professor Bernard Crick, a 'full history of the institution of opposition in Britain has still to be written'.

The growth of 'organized opposition'

There was 'opposition' during the first half of the eighteenth century, but opposition to the actions of the Crown and the Ministers of the Crown, court favourites versus anti-courtiers, rather than organized party opposition as we know it today in Parliament and the country. 'Parties' or groups were numerous and everchanging in their allegiances and often the chance of a government office or sinecure was sufficient to lure members of the so-called 'opposition' into active co-operation with the government of the day. The 'opposition' consisted of groups of shifting alliances of nobles and followers temporarily out of favour at Court. These motley gatherings were often called 'coalitions' or 'camarillas' as, for example, those formed by Bolingbroke and William Pulteney and later Pulteney and Carteret. Meetings were held to discuss policy and tactics at the London town houses or country estates of many of these leading figures. However, as Professor Foord admits when reviewing the period 1715-1725 in his recent work on the Opposition, 'no specific contract bound its (the Opposition) members and within its counsels there lurked no Shadow Cabinet' (Foord, 120).

During the latter part of the eighteenth century, Parliament witnessed a period of virulent opposition with the contributions of Fox, Burke and their Whig colleagues;

2

though even then, what may be termed party lines were very fluid indeed, Whig support being divided between Rockingham, on the one hand, and the other, Chatham and Shelburne. At this time the so-called 'Rockinghamites' held what have since been called 'conciliabula', meetings of an inner council of leading members of the group to discuss policy and tactics, though not upon any regular basis. Meetings were usually convened at moments of party crisis, the group possessing the services of a 'party whip' who was an important figure in the organization during a session.

To be really effective, Opposition parties, by the very nature of their existence, require important issues upon which to oppose. In 1774, the start of the war with America provided just such an issue. Burke delivered his speeches on 'American Taxation' and 'Conciliation', whilst Fox displayed his talents as a debater, though even now opposition remained largely unorganized. Success was usually short-lived. A powerful and emotive speech could often disconcert and embarrass the Ministry. This, of course, was good for opposition morale but had little real effect upon those in power, a point well illustrated by the secession of the 'Rockinghamites' in 1776. When war broke out with France some two years later, Fox was again very forthright in his attacks upon Government, apparently mustering some 160 votes in the division following his speech on 2 February 1778. The Whigs continued to attack the Government, with varying degrees of success, right up to 1782 when North resigned. There was still little or no evidence to suggest, however, that any Shadow Cabinet organization was in operation. It seemed to matter little who was actually in Opposition. For example, during the period of the Fox-North coalition in 1783, Pitt's opposition has been described as 'vehement but ineffective' (Foord, 392).

If there was no Shadow Cabinet in existence, and this seems fairly obvious, the stage was slowly being set from the middle of the eighteenth century onwards. The anti-courtiers referred to a little earlier began to be written about as the 'opposition' from 1731 onwards and also began to sit on the Speaker's left in the House of Commons. It has also been suggested that the term 'opposition' may well have arisen out of the fact that they sat *opposite* the Treasury benches. Evidently, the expression, 'opposite party' was, in fact, used during this period (ibid., 155-9).

Undoubtedly, the greatest obstacle which the Opposition had to surmount was that of its constitutional right to exist at all. As Sir Ivor Jennings has pointed out, for the larger part of the eighteenth century the idea of political opposition was taken to mean opposition to the Crown and hence unconstitutional. The political situation in Europe did little to enhance the standing of the Opposition in Britain, any form of political gathering being looked upon with distrust and even fear. The situation was aggravated still further by the operation of the reversionary interest, a practice whereby the Opposition tended to centre itself around the court of the Prince of Wales. This could, and often did, lead to bitterness between King and Prince who regarded themselves as rivals for power. The relationships between George III and the Prince of Wales, for example, appear to have been somewhat tenuous, the latter intriguing with Fox and the Opposition during the period of the King's illness in 1788. Indeed, in his very interesting account of the 'Regency Crisis', J. W. Derry often refers to meetings of Opposition 'councils' at which the Prince of Wales was present, including one such gathering to which Burke was summoned at Lord Loughborough's in February 1789 (Derry, 165). Apparently, lists of 'new' or 'shadow' Ministers and Peers were even in circulation but, as the doctors had predicted, George recovered and in the 1790 election his Ministers were returned victorious.

The beginning of the nineteenth century did not herald any major developments in the history of the Shadow

Cabinet, Opposition still appearing to be based around cliques and cabals with no visible 'collective responsibility' or appointment procedure. However, recent research indicates that there were differences in regard to the standing of the party leader, who was felt to be 'less important than his counterparts, either before or since'. It is argued that, whereas eighteenth-century cliques and cabals centred on one man, who was often the 'raison d'etre of the group', the early nineteenth-century Whig leader was the first among equals, the head of a coalition of faction leaders (Mitchell, 25-6).

Nevertheless, as J. P. Mackintosh has pointed out, it was becoming increasingly necessary to *attempt* to work together as a team.

Quasi-cabinets

Quite a number of what may be termed Opposition 'councils' were convened by the Whig leaders during the period of their opposition after 1807. These gatherings sometimes included upwards of forty members, but more often consisted of smaller 'councils' between the various leaders to discuss parliamentary tactics and aspects of policy. During this period of Whig Opposition, considerable trouble and confusion centred around the question of party leadership in the House of Commons. Much of this trouble stemmed from the fact that two peers, Grenville, who retired in 1812, and then Grey, acted as overall leaders of the Whigs. Lord Grey seemed particularly indifferent to the duties of leadership, yet declined until 1825 either to play a more vigorous role or to retire entirely from the scene. Apart from the effect upon the party as a whole, Grey's indifferent leadership posed undoubted difficulties for Ponsonby, the leader in the Commons.

When Ponsonby died in 1817, after ten arduous years of leading the Whigs in the Commons, considerable doubts were expressed as to whether the post should be filled at all, many feeling that no acceptable candidates were available. It was at this juncture that Lord Althorp apparently put forward a scheme whereby a committee of some twenty persons would be elected by a ballot of members of the party. This committee would control the affairs of the party and from its membership a leader would 'emerge' (Mitchell, 30-2). Though the scheme did not prove successful it bears striking resemblances to the elected 'Parliamentary Committee' and Shadow Cabinet established by the Parliamentary Labour Party some one hundred and six years later.

When Tierney finally emerged as leader in July 1818, it was largely thanks to the efforts of the party Whip, Duncannon, who, according to Mitchell, organized with the assistance of Sefton a letter signed by over one hundred M.P.'s asking Tierney to accept the leadership. Following a short but successful period as leader in the Commons, Tierney's health broke down and he withdrew from the leadership early in 1821. There followed renewed debate about the leadership issue, Lord John Russell, apparently, urging the setting up of what amounted to a Shadow Cabinet. His proposal involved the establishment of a 'committee' of from seven to ten members which would, in his own words, 'be a sort of cabinet'. Russell considered such a scheme necessary, in a party of some two hundred members, to bind different opinions together and put business into some form prior to general meetings (Mitchell, 36-7). The proposals of both Althorp and Russell definitely appear to be two of the earliest formalized attempts to establish a Shadow Cabinet within the ranks of the parliamentary opposition.

J. P. Mackintosh refers to meetings of 'quasi-cabinets' which the group known as the 'Stanleyites' held after leaving the Whig ministry of Grey in 1834, though these cannot really be called meetings of a Shadow Cabinet. They were simply meetings of the small group of supporters, admittedly ex-Ministers, of Edward Stanley who could not reconcile their views upon the question of the confiscation of Irish Church revenues with those of the remainder of the Government. James Graham's letters nowhere indicate the existence of a Shadow Cabinet, other than a meeting with Stanley at Knowsley Park on 21 November 1834, together with Richmond, at which all three agreed to decline any offer to serve under Peel and later at what was called, a 'Cabinet' at Goodwood, this time arranged by Richmond (Parker, i, 214-24).

During the very early part of 1835, Melbourne, in Opposition himself to Peel, apparently settled the policy of the Whigs together with a small 'committee' which included Lansdowne, Russell, Spring, Rice and Hobhouse (Mackintosh, 142). Melbourne was not long out of office. The year 1836 saw Peel leading the Opposition and, as we have seen above, calling a meeting of his principal colleagues to discuss discipline.

Whilst the proposals put forward by Althorp and Russell in the early 1820s and the subsequent meetings held by Stanley and Melbourne were, undoubtedly, early examples of an emerging Shadow Cabinet system, it would be unwise to assume that they represented stages in a logical progression towards such a system. Indeed, a Liberal leader as knowledgeable as Sir William Harcourt could still argue and deny the existence of any Shadow Cabinet as late as 1876.

Peel and his colleagues were to remain in Opposition for some five years, returning to office at the end of August 1841. The development of organized opposition and the Shadow Cabinet, as mentioned earlier, has followed no clear pattern, depending rather more upon the effectiveness of the Ministry in office and the attitudes of those in Opposition. It thus appears that there was a lack of co-ordinated opposition to Peel and his colleagues between 1841-6. However, the Government, particularly during the last year of its tenure of office, contained the elements of its own destruction, Peel dividing the Tories into two halves over the repeal of the Corn Laws. One hundred and twelve 'Peelites' supported the action of their leader, whilst Lord George Bentinck and Disraeli led a determined and, at times, vociferous attack upon their former leader, finally forcing his resignation by combining with the Whigs to defeat the Second Reading of the Irish Coercion Bill.

Following Peel's defeat, the Queen sent for Lord John Russell. As Robert Blake has pointed out, it was to be twenty-eight years before a Conservative Prime Minister again headed a ministry with a clear majority in the House of Commons.

The years between 1846 and 1860 were uneasy and confused ones for those in Opposition, with very little evidence to support the existence of a Shadow Cabinet, though Disraeli, writing to Lady Londonderry in December 1846, claimed that his party had a 'better chance of governing the country than the *late Cabinet*' (Monypenny & Buckle, i, 827). The occasional meeting did, of course, take place. For example, Disraeli refers to meetings of a 'Cabinet' at Burleigh House in January 1850, attended by Stanley and Granby, at which political discourse was suitably interspersed with some shooting. Other leading figures present at this gathering included Richmond, Sandwich, Southampton, Inglis, Herries, Christopher, H. Bentinck, Trollope, Maunsell, Stafford and the Whip, Beresford (Monypenny & Buckle, i 1056). During the period of the Aberdeen Coalition from 1852-5, Disraeli refers to 'dissentions in our Cabinet', whilst there was also at least one meeting of what was called a 'Cabinet Council' at Knowsley Park on 10 December 1853, attended by Derby, Malmesbury, Hardwicke and Disraeli (Malmesbury, 317).

Twice during this period, in 1851 and again in 1855, Lord Derby failed to form an administration. To modern observers it seems inconceivable that an Opposition, after defeating the Government, could be so unprepared for office. Commenting upon the whole affair Sir John Pakington felt that: 'if we (the Opposition) go on treating Ministers like ninepins—only bowling them down to set them up again—we shall be bowled down ourselves'. Derby's failure to form a Government in 1855 both annoyed and upset the Conservatives, in particular Disraeli who, according to Malmesbury, was in 'a state of disgust beyond all control'. Derby later explained to his party that the possible candidates for inclusion in his Government had been tried in Opposition and found wanting both in ability and experience, an argument many found difficult to accept.

Disraeli's approach to the question of parliamentary opposition during these years differed considerably from those held by Derby. As Robert Blake rightly points out, 'Disraeli's first instinct was to oppose and, if he did not always do so, it was for reasons of expediency or because Derby overruled him' (Blake, 1966, 355). In fact, many people now consider that Disraeli established the precedent that it is the duty of the Opposition to oppose. This may well be correct, but he most certainly did not make any extensive use of a Shadow Cabinet, preferring instead to spend many hours upon proposals for reforming the structure of the Cabinet.

'The Cabinet of the Opposition'

Meetings of the Shadow Cabinet, or at least records of such meetings, appear to be very few and far between. Jolliffe, the Chief Whip, refers to meetings of 'small cabinets' formed from both Houses of Parliament in 1856. Malmesbury refers to a meeting of Opposition leaders at Lord Eglinton's on 7 May 1857, to discuss the Queen's speech (Malmesbury, 350), whilst the Gathorne Hardy memoirs include references to meetings of 'informal cabinets' following the Conservatives' return to Opposition in 1859. These meetings, which Gathorne Hardy was regularly invited to attend, were composed of between

9

ten and twelve persons and were called at times of political crisis.

The fusion of Whigs, Liberals, Radicals and Peelites which had brought about the downfall of the very short-lived Derby Government in 1859 meant that Derby, Disraeli and their colleagues were destined to spend some six years in Opposition. These years, as Robert Blake points out, were 'comparatively uneventful' ones for Disraeli, though he did take a very active interest in foreign affairs. As is so often the case with a party recently returned to Opposition, there was a certain body of opinion critical of Disraeli's actions, blaming him for the Conservative defeat in 1859, though this soon evaporated. Within the walls of Parliament, Derby and Disraeli even went so far as to conclude a parliamentary truce with Palmerston, an arrangement which was to last until the middle of 1864. The issue upon which the truce finally foundered was the Government's handling of the Schleswig-Holstein affair. As in the case of the other important foreign issues of the period, including the American Civil War, Disraeli favoured a policy of non-intervention, a course not always popular with his colleagues, who discussed the issue fully at what was called 'the Cabinet of the Opposition' which met at Lord Derby's home in June 1864 (Gathorne Hardy, i, 137-42).

It may still be argued, of course, that these meetings, like those referred to in the eighteenth and early nineteenth centuries, were not meetings of the 'Shadow Cabinet' in the modern sense of the word. This is the problem. One is constantly tempted to think in terms of the modern Shadow Cabinet with its relatively formalized structure and procedure. However the above examples illustrate that there was, undoubtedly, a modified form of Shadow Cabinet in existence by 1860.

2
Shadow Cabinets emerge

By the second half of the nineteenth century, gatherings of ex-Cabinet Ministers had thus begun to appear on the political scene. These meetings, or conclaves, still consisted of comparatively small numbers of persons, particularly in view of modern experience, although those referred to by Gathorne Hardy did often contain between ten to twelve persons.

Party divisions were also becoming more clearly defined, the struggle being basically reduced to one between the Conservatives and the Liberals, or perhaps more correctly, to one between two outstanding figures, Gladstone and Disraeli, with a third force looming ominously on the sidelines, namely the Irish and the question of Home Rule. This issue was to affect all parties and split the Liberal ranks asunder in the not too distant future.

Opposition still in disarray

Whilst Opposition meetings, or 'quasi Shadow Cabinets' were undoubtedly held, they were not on any regular weekly or monthly basis. Special meetings had to be called to resolve problems as and when they arose. Some of the commonest gatherings were those held between a small number of the leaders to discuss and decide the possible composition of a potential Cabinet or Government. There was also a considerable amount of haggling over the distribution of offices, thereby providing fairly conclusive evidence that members of the Opposition were not yet 'shadowing' specific offices. This general lack of organization seems to have been widely prevalent during the mid-nineteenth century and Mackintosh, for example, refers to a number of instances where rapid consultations were held between leading members of a prospective administration prior to accepting office, including meetings held by such leaders as Russell and Derby.

One of the main purposes of a Shadow Cabinet is to ensure that there is, within limits, an alternative team ready to take office, a team which has had the opportunity of working together in Opposition. This eliminates, to some extent, the doubt and uncertainty over the distribution of posts, particularly the major offices of state. A number of Ministers in the 1866 Derby Cabinet had, in fact, worked together in Opposition during 1865. Furthermore, their contributions were often on subjects closely related to their subsequent ministerial portfolios. For example, Lord Stanley, the Foreign Secretary, took part in debates and questions about India, Africa and New Zealand, whilst Sir J. Pakington (First Lord of the Admiralty) took a prominent part in all discussions concerned with the Royal Navy. Sir Stafford Northcote (President, Board of Trade) took part in the Select Committee on Trade with Foreign Nations, whilst General Peel (War Secretary) spoke regularly on the Army Estimates and other military matters (H.C. Debates, 3s, Vols. 177-80, 1865).

Derby had formed his 1866 Cabinet after the resignation of Russell, who had become Prime Minister once again following the death of Palmerston in 1865; with Russell in the House of Lords, Gladstone led in the Commons. The Government had been defeated on the question of franchise reform, Russell's Bill being opposed not only by the Conservatives but also by some thirty Liberals led by Robert Lowe.

In 1867, Disraeli himself introduced a franchise bill, thereby, in the words of Lord Derby, 'dishing the Whigs' over the question of reform. This reversal of roles, as Ivor Bulmer-Thomas has pointed out, was a definite feature of the period between the 1834 and 1867 Reform Acts, with Tory measures often being carried by Whig governments and *vice versa* (Bulmer-Thomas, i, 102-12).

What was the reaction of Gladstone and the Liberal Opposition in the House of Commons to this new situation? This was clearly not the time to oppose the Government simply for the sake of opposing, but Gladstone appears to have been a little doubtful as to the nature of Disraeli's bill. In a letter to Mr Speaker Brand on 30 October 1866, Gladstone stated that 'a good bill from them (the Conservatives) would save us much trouble and anxiety . . . but their bill will be neither good nor straightforward. . . . We may have to meet a tortuous bill by a tortuous motion. This is what I am afraid of, and what I am, for one, above all things anxious to avoid' (Morley, i, 856-7).

The leadership issue

Gladstone did, in fact, attack the bill when it was introduced in March 1867, but following a meeting of some 278 Liberals at his house, Gladstone agreed, unwillingly, that the Party would not oppose the bill at Second Reading. The Government were, to use Gladstone's own words, 'masters of the situation' and the 1867 Bill passed into law with little or no real opposition. However, Gladstone's leadership had met with opposition, though not, it seems, from members of his 'late Cabinet' who remained loyal. On 11 April 1867 Gladstone had moved an amendment to remove the personal payment of rates as an essential qualification and also to confer the franchise

13

on the householder whether he paid the rate direct or through the landlord. This amendment had been defeated by 310 votes to 289, some 43 Liberals voting with the Government and a further 20 being absent from the House. Following this defeat, Gladstone, both 'disgusted and mortified', called what can only be described as a meeting of the Shadow Cabinet. Five or six members of the 'late Cabinet' were summoned to his house and he expressed in strong terms his feelings on the whole matter, indicating that he considered retiring to a back-bench and announcing that he 'would give up the ostensible post of leader of the opposition' (Morley, i, 867). This he was dissuaded from doing, though the threat had been quite effective in mustering his supporters behind him.

During 1868 Gladstone again held meetings with former ministerial colleagues. According to Mackintosh, Gladstone called together six such colleagues in March, namely Argyle, Granville, Fortescue, Cardwell, Brand and Glynne, in order to discuss the Irish Church. It appears that similar meetings were held at regular intervals during May and, in addition, Gladstone consulted with, at a more informal level, even smaller numbers of the inner circle within the 'late Cabinet' or Shadow Cabinet (Mackintosh, 248-9). By December 1868 Gladstone was back in office at the head of a Liberal administration that was to last until 1874.

Disraeli had become Prime Minister in February 1868 following the resignation through ill health of Lord Derby. The new leader in the House of Lords was Richmond, two clear candidates, Salisbury and the new Lord Derby standing down in favour of this compromise third candidate. The Prime Minister, hoping perhaps to gain wide support from the newly enfranchised voters, decided to dissolve in the autumn of 1868. The result of the Election was, instead, a 112-seat majority for the Liberals.

Following defeat, Disraeli set about putting the Conservative Party machine on an efficient footing, a development which has since followed all major Conservative electoral defeats. However, no such approach was forthcoming at Westminster. Disraeli still persisted with his non-aggressive approach towards the Gladstone administration, employing 'the utmost reserve and quietness' in all his actions. The argument put forward in favour of this approach to the tasks of opposition was that little use could be derived from fighting against a large ministerial majority. 'Her Majesty's Opposition' could put up little more than token resistance and was, therefore, of little practical use. It appears that Disraeli took the opportunity thus provided to focus his attention upon leisure and his 'early love', literature (Monypenny and Buckle, ii, 488).

In just the same way as had occurred between 1859 and 1866, elements of the party soon began to agitate quite vigorously for more action against the Government rather than waiting for it to commit suicide (Monypenny and Buckle, ii, 511-13). A meeting was held at the house of the Marquis of Exeter in January 1872, attended by Gathorne Hardy, Lord Cairns, Pakington, Hay, Hunt, Lord John Manners, the Duke of Marlborough, Lord Eustace Cecil, Gerald Noel and Sir Stafford Northcote (Gathorne Hardy, i, 300). By April, however Disraeli was firmly back in the saddle, if indeed he had ever been out of it, without any really apparent changes in his tactics.

The year 1873 was to witness a long and complicated constitutional wrangle between Gladstone and Disraeli. In March, Gladstone decided to resign after the Liberals had been defeated on the Irish University Bill by 284 votes to 287. Disraeli, however, seemed loathe to accept office and declined to undertake the formation of a Government, Gladstone finally having to carry on until early 1874. The whole episode was rather unusual. The Conservatives had been in Opposition since late 1868 and yet did not, apparently, wish to accept office in these circumstances. According to Morley, the vote had been a clear party issue on which the Government had nailed its colours. In the words of Mr Speaker Brand, 'Disraeli's tactics were to watch and wait, not showing his hand nor declaring a policy'. The intention was to drive Gladstone to a dissolution (Morley, ii, 55-64).

Disraeli's laxity in Opposition was taken to the extreme position of not even possessing a party manifesto prior to taking office in 1874. Apparently, when he heard that Gladstone had advised the Queen to dissolve Parliament in January of that year, Disraeli found himself willing but completely unprepared for the challenge. In Disraeli's own words, 'a political manifesto is the most responsible of all undertakings, and I had not a human being to share that responsibility' (Monypenny and Buckle, ii, 612). It should be noted in Disraeli's defence that this situation occurred during the Christmas recess, some two weeks prior to the opening of the new Session. The Opposition colleagues whom Disraeli summoned with all haste to London were Lords Derby and Cairns, Gathorne Hardy and Sir Stafford Northcote, together with the Leader's Secretary, Montague Corry. There was little or no hesitation in placing ex-Ministers in their old Departments, Cairns, Malmesbury, Derby, Carnarvon and Salisbury returning to the respective offices of Lord Chancellor, Lord Privy Seal, Foreign Secretary, Colonial Secretary and Indian Secretary.

Following the 1874 dissolution and the installation of the Conservatives under Disraeli, Gladstone decided to retire from the leadership. He was reported to be tired of the bickering which had continued throughout the latter stages of the former administration. Gladstone's decision came as a considerable shock both to the leaders and the rank and file members of the party and there was confusion as to who would lead the Opposition in the future. Prior to his handing over the reins of 'office', and the sharing of the duties of Opposition leadership between Granville and Hartington, Gladstone called together a number of members of 'his 'late Government'. Those present included Granville, Halifax, Cardwell, Hartington,

Aberdare, Forster, Carlingford, Stansfeld, Selborne, Goschen, Lowe and Kimberley, the absentees being Argyle and Bright (Morley, ii, 112).

Gladstone's *'retirement'* could not really claim to be anything more than partial and he continued to sit upon the Opposition Front Bench where he proved to be quite a source of embarrassment to the party leadership on more than one occasion. Indeed, the whole episode proved awkward for all concerned. Gladstone remained the most influential figure in the whole party, the majority still looking upon him as their natural leader. This, obviously, caused difficulties for the 'substitute leadership' of Hartington and Granville. Gladstone's position was most aptly described by the diarist H. W. Lucy as being 'such another withdrawal from the conduct of affairs as the captain of a ship effects when he turns in for the night'. Referring to the same subject, Hartington was convinced that the leadership of the party should reside with the party as a whole and not with individuals or 'by the dictation of the late Cabinet'. This somewhat impractical suggestion was contained in a letter sent by Hartington to Sir William Harcourt in January 1875. In his letter, Hartington refers to the Opposition consisting of Whigs, Radicals and Home Rulers, all of whom were pulling in different directions (Gardiner, i, 289).

Sir William Harcourt and the Shadow Cabinet

The following year, Sir William Harcourt himself objected to the Liberal Shadow Cabinet deciding the policy of the Opposition led by Hartington and Granville. Apparently Harcourt and Sir Henry James, both of whom had been law officers under Gladstone, were summoned to a Shadow Cabinet meeting to consider the Slave Circular, a document of current controversy, but not other matters.

Harcourt declined to attend the Shadow Cabinet meeting and wrote a letter of protest to Hartington which provides us with perhaps the most powerful indictment of the whole Shadow Cabinet system ever written. Harcourt protested against the 'exclusive pretensions of the gentlemen who call themselves the "late Cabinet" to direct and control the policy of the Opposition'. The former Solicitor General knew nothing of the 'late Cabinet' which, in his opinion, had been dissolved by the election of 1874. Pressing home his attack still further, Sir William stated that 'he did not know who was the author of the dogma that the leader of the Opposition was to consult only with ex-Cabinet Ministers on the general policy of the Party'. In his opinion, there was no such rule and had never been any such practice. It was a 'novelty and a solecism in politics' (Gardiner, i, 300-1).

The remaining years of the Liberal Opposition up to 1880 were to witness numbers of such gatherings of the Liberal hierarchy; meetings were called at times of crisis or at the beginning of a new Session of Parliament, rather than on any regular and permanent basis. For example, on the day prior to the new Session in February 1877, such a meeting was held at Lord Granville's home attended by, amongst others, Harcourt, Argyle, Gladstone, Hartington and Forster (Gardiner, i, 317). It is thus fair to say that the concept of the 'Shadow Cabinet' had become a recognized part of the British political machine by the second half of the nineteenth century, though its use was still limited and its full potential unrecognized.

3
A steady development

With the return to office of the Liberals in 1880, led officially by Gladstone, the Opposition comprised the Conservatives with the addition of those aggressive supporters of Parnell who were fighting for Irish Home Rule. Opposition became more militant. Parnell developed the practice of destructive and obstructive Opposition to the full, whilst Randolph Churchill and the so-called 'Fourth Party' adopted fierce and aggressive methods which evidently disregarded all the conventions of parliamentary practice. Gladstone did not approve of such tactics, placing the blame fairly and squarely upon the shoulders of Disraeli whom he described as the 'grand corrupter' (Morley, ii, 715). Disraeli had, in fact, been removed to the House of Lords in 1876, the affairs of the Lower House being left in the hands of Sir Stafford Northcote, though Disraeli remained overall Leader of the Conservatives.

The Bradlaugh affair was a source of considerable friction at this time. The issue revolved around whether Bradlaugh, an atheist, could make an affirmation rather than take an oath upon taking his seat in Parliament. Lord Beaconsfield attended a meeting of Conservative leaders on 24 June 1880, to discuss this matter. The meeting was held at the home of Ridley and was attended also by Cranbrook (Gathorne Hardy), Cross, Smith, Lord John

Manners, Sandon, Beach, Holker, Gibson and Sir Stafford
Northcote (Lang, 329). The ageing leader also held a large
meeting on 8 August 1880 to discuss the Ground Game
Bill, and a further meeting of the 'Old Cabinet' on 23
February 1881, to discuss the state of affairs in the House
of Commons. The Cranbrook diary records two further
meetings with Lord Beaconsfield, the first on 11 March
1881, when the Shadow Cabinet discussed finance and on
26 March 1881, when Beaconsfield saw Salisbury, Cairns
and Cranbrook (Gathorne Hardy, ii, 142-57).

Opposition led in the Commons by Northcote

Following Lord Beaconsfield's death, the Conservatives
divided the leadership between Lord Salisbury in the
House of Lords and Sir Stafford Northcote, who had been
re-elected by the Conservative M.P.s in the House of
Commons. It appears that Northcote was somewhat over-
awed by Gladstone, having previously been his private
secretary at the Board of Trade, the main assault upon
the Government being carried out by Randolph Churchill
and his 'Fourth Party' colleagues Sir Henry Drummond
Wolff, John Gorst and, upon occasions, Arthur Balfour
(Magnus, 274-5).

Most observers agree that Northcote was a weak Leader
in the House of Commons. His biographer, Andrew Lang,
was less critical than most, but even he informs us that
'the exercise of authority gave Sir Stafford Northcote no
pleasure at all' (Lang, 309-10). As leader, he did not consider it worthwhile to be constantly on the attack, preferring to choose his moments for an Opposition challenge
with considerable care. His approach was constantly compared with that of Churchill and his colleagues who
appeared so much more forward-looking and vigorous.
It was not surprising, therefore, that Salisbury, the other
half of the leadership duumvirate in the Conservative
party, began to play an increasingly dominant role in

20

the decision-making process. When the Liberal Government was defeated in 1885, the Queen sent for Lord Salisbury in preference to Sir Stafford Northcote.

During the tenure of his leadership of the party in the House of Commons, Sir Stafford Northcote held a number of meetings with his Conservative colleagues to discuss party policy and other issues of importance. Lord Carnarvon attended a 'private meeting' with Northcote in August 1881 to discuss the Land Bill, whilst Cranbrook refers to meetings of the 'Old Cabinet' in May 1882 (Hardinge, iii, 114). Two further meetings of the 'Old Cabinet' were held in the autumn of 1884, the first on 22 October at Arlington Street to discuss tactics prior to the meeting of Parliament and the second at the Carlton Club on 18 November, when the issue under discussion was the redistribution of parliamentary seats (Gathorne Hardy, ii, 199; Hardinge, iii, 118). It is very likely that there were many more meetings held than those actually referred to in the letters and diaries of the leading figures in Opposition, but such evidence is scarce.

Gladstone and the Shadow Cabinet

Following Gladstone's defeat in June 1885 at the combined hands of the Conservatives and the Irish, he declined to call meetings of his old Cabinet colleagues, despite requests by Harcourt, of all people, feeling that little good would come of them (Mackintosh, 248-9). Granville supported Gladstone on this matter, stating that he had declined requests for the convening of such a meeting to discuss the state of affairs in the party. In his reply to Granville, Gladstone stated that he did not consider that a cabinet existed out of office, and that 'no one in his senses could covenant to call the "late cabinet" together' (Morley, ii, 509). When the election was finally held in the Autumn of 1885, Government and Opposition emerged numerically equal, the Conservatives with 249 seats, supported by Parnell and 86 Home Rulers, opposed by Gladstone and 335 Liberals. The Irish were now in a most powerful position and when, early in 1886, Salisbury's Cabinet failed to proceed with their intention to assist the Irish towards a greater degree of Home Rule and reverted instead to a policy of coercion, Parnell withdrew his support from the Conservatives. On 27 January following an amendment to the address, the Government was defeated, the Opposition mustering some 331 votes, which included 74 Irish nationalist votes, to the Government's 252 votes (Morley, ii, 528).

The return to the ranks of the Opposition by Salisbury and his colleagues was to be very short-lived, the Liberal Government lasting some six months from February until August 1886, after which they, in turn, handed over the reins of office. The brief duration of Gladstone's third Ministry was dominated by one issue, namely the 1886 Irish Home Rule Bill. Gladstone must have fully realized the magnitude of the task before him in championing the 1886 Home Rule Bill. Queen Victoria was opposed to the measure, as were a number of prominent Whigs led by Hartington who had, in fact, declined to join the Government. It appears that others, including Trevelyan and Chamberlain expressed serious doubts about the proposed legislation and when Gladstone presented his Bill to the Cabinet, both men resigned. It transpired that Gladstone undertook the entire drafting of the Bill himself without seeking the advice or guidance of any of his senior colleagues (Bulmer-Thomas, i, 139).

The Liberals in trouble: Chamberlain departs

The schism in the Liberal ranks widened once the party had returned to Opposition, Harcourt apparently working hard for a reconciliation between Chamberlain and the remainder of the party, though to no avail (Morley, ii, 509-10). Gladstone had declined to resign following his

22

defeat in the House of Commons, preferring to take the issue to the country in an election, where he was also defeated. Following the 1886 Home Rule crisis, Chamberlain and a number of dissentient Liberals entered into a compact with the Conservatives. This group, which soon became known as the Liberal Unionists, gradually drew further apart from the remainder of the Liberal party, finally being absorbed into the ranks of the Conservative party.

Gladstone and his colleagues were to remain in Opposition for some six years, returning to office in August 1892. Shortly after the seventy-seven-year-old leader had resigned office he left for a vacation at Tegernsee in Bavaria together with Lord Acton. Gladstone maintained the closest contacts with Sir William Harcourt who was, undoubtedly, one of the leading figures in Opposition during this period as well as being one of the most loyal supporters of the Liberal party. Sir William took charge of the Opposition in the absence of his leader and he led determined attacks against the Government on a wide range of subjects, challenging Balfour on Ireland, Goschen on finance, Ritchie on local government and Chamberlain on 'anything and everything' (Gardiner, ii, 102). Harcourt's closest associate during these years in Opposition was John Morley though, apart from correspondence with Gladstone, there appears to have been very little contact with any wider group of colleagues. There is very little mention of meetings of any Shadow Cabinet during these years, though this is not hard to understand in the light of Harcourt's opinions upon the question of Shadow Cabinets uttered some sixteen years previously over the Slave Circular issue.

Almost the entire period of Liberal Opposition between 1886 and 1892 was taken up with the Irish issue, in which Gladstone was deeply involved. Indeed, national attention was focused upon the affairs of Ireland and, more particularly, upon the person of the Irish leader at Westminster,

Parnell. However Gladstone did find sufficient time and energy to spend two recuperative vacations in Italy, leaving the affairs of the Liberal party in the hands of his trusted lieutenant, Harcourt. Whilst meetings of the Shadow Cabinet appear to have been infrequent during this period, both men did attend such a gathering in June 1890 and there was also a conference of Liberal leaders in December 1891 at Lord Spencer's house, attended by Gladstone, Harcourt, J. Morley and Rosebery (Gardiner, ii, 150-60).

John Morley and the Shadow Cabinet

A most interesting incident took place just prior to the opening of the Session in February 1892. It would seem that there was a 'semi-official' dinner for the leaders of the Liberal party. Morley declined Harcourt's invitation to attend this gathering. In his reply, which gives some indication of the growing stature of the Shadow Cabinet as a part of the British political machine, Harcourt stated that the dinner was in 'the nature of a Cabinet dinner, which by the British Constitution overrides all engagements'. He referred to the 'sinister rumours' to which Morley's absence upon such occasion would give rise amongst the 'well-informed London correspondents' (Gardiner, ii, 168). Harcourt's comments indicate that the press would have regarded Morley's absence from this Opposition function as a breach in the Shadow Cabinet, thereby indicating the existence of some principle of collective unity or responsibility upon the part of the members of this body. Early in the Session of 1892, the Liberal Shadow Cabinet did, in fact, find itself divided. The issue under discussion was a private bill concerned with miners' hours of work. Morley, on the one hand, had to oppose it since miners in his constituency were against the bill, whilst Harcourt had to take into account the wishes of miners in his constituency who were not opposed to the measure (Gardiner, ii, 171).

Despite meetings of Shadow Cabinets and other smaller gatherings of the Opposition hierarchy, trouble often arose in selecting a Cabinet. The position of the Liberals in July and August 1892 was no exception. Prominent members of the Opposition were normally included in any sub-sequent Cabinet, but this did not exclude the considerable amount of haggling over the actual distribution of offices. For example, Gladstone and Harcourt disagreed over the distribution of important posts between the House of Commons and the Lords (Gardiner, ii, 178-85). Gladstone, Rosebery and John Morley spent hours at Dalmeny Park in Scotland considering the composition of a Liberal administration. However, there was no such difficulty with Morley himself, who, when asked about his own office, 'fancied like Regulus that he had better go back to the Irish department' (Morley, ii, 731). To this, Gladstone readily agreed. Gladstone formed his fourth and last administration in August 1892, the Liberals retaining power until the middle of 1895, though the Prime Minister himself retired in March 1894. During this period, the Conservative Opposition in the House of Commons was led by Balfour, apparently being in cheerful and truculent mood when Parliament met in January 1893 (Dugdale, i, 214).

Opposition responsibilities and Ministerial appointments

One of the basic points about the modern Shadow Cabinet is that members of this body specialize and take responsi-bility in Opposition for particular subjects. It has become quite common for many of these shadow spokesmen, either upon the entry of their party to office, or upon their return to the role of Opposition, to be given responsi-bility for a particular subject or Department. Did any similar relationships between Opposition and Cabinet

responsibilities operate during the latter part of the nineteenth century? We have seen already that there was
some slight relationship between the allocation of portfolios in the 1866 Derby Cabinet and those who spoke
from the Opposition Front Bench during the 1865 Session
of Parliament. During the period of Conservative Opposition between 1893 and 1895, numbers of ex-Ministers,
particularly during the earlier months of Opposition continued to speak from the Opposition benches on their
former departments. It is still difficult, however, to identify
any organized pattern of Front Bench spokesmen
'shadowing' specific subjects over any period of time.

The attention of Parliament was often turned during
these years to the seemingly insoluble problem of Ireland
and her relationships with Westminster. For example, the
Government of Ireland Bill was debated at great length
throughout 1893. Sir E. Clarke, one of the ex-law officers,
opening for the Opposition on 13 February, Balfour resum-
ing the adjourned debate the following day, followed by
Lord Randolph Churchill on the 16th and Joseph Chamberlain on the 17th of the month (H.C. Debates, 4s, Vol.
VIII). The Committee stage of the Bill continued through
May, June and July, the debate on Second Reading being
concluded on 8 September 1893.

On matters other than Ireland, Viscount Cross, the
former Secretary of State for India, spoke often on matters
concerning that country. Stanhope, the ex-Secretary of
State for War, spoke, until his death later in 1893, on
army questions as did Chaplin, the ex-President of the
Board of Agriculture, on matters concerning that subject.
Lord George Hamilton, the ex-First Lord of the Admiralty,
spoke on naval matters, Sir William Hart-Dyke on education and W. H. Long on matters concerning local government (H.C. Debates, 4s, Vols. VIII to XX). That ex-
Ministers, for a while at least, should continue to speak
on their Departments was only natural. It did not mean
that those men were, upon the return of their party to

power, once more given responsibility for their old Departments. Of those Ministers who sat in the 1886-92 Salisbury Cabinet, fourteen were asked to serve in 1895, a high proportion, though only four, Salisbury himself, Halsbury, Balfour and Ashbourne retained their old portfolios.

Campbell-Bannerman becomes Leader of the Opposition

At the 1895 election the Liberals were reduced from 274 to 177 seats, losing both Harcourt and John Morley. Apparently, Lord Spencer called for a meeting of the Liberal Shadow Cabinet in August 1895 to discuss the party leadership and the conduct of the election campaign in which both Harcourt and Morley had failed to follow the Rosebery line, the latter having succeeded Gladstone in 1894 (Spender and Asquith, i, 112-16). Rosebery decided not to continue his association with Harcourt, a decision which came as quite a shock both to Harcourt and other senior ex-Ministers (Gardiner, ii, 375-7). It seemed for a time that the Liberal Opposition would be left leaderless but, finally, an agreement was reached whereby Harcourt, who soon found another parliamentary seat, and Kimberley shared the leadership responsibilities in the two Houses, though Rosebery did not officially resign until December 1896. Sir William Harcourt resigned two years later, followed in January 1899 by his colleague of so many years standing, John Morley. Three names were put forward as successors to Harcourt as Opposition leader in the House of Commons, Asquith, H. H. Fowler and Campbell-Bannerman, the last named emerging to assume that title with its attendant trials and tribulations in February 1899.

The new Leader was chosen by the Shadow Cabinet which, to use Asquith's own words, was 'restricted to communicant ex-Cabs'. It would appear that there was some question as to how many Front Benchers should be consulted about the choice of Leader, Tweedmouth, a former Chief Whip, preferring a meeting of *all* Front Benchers, a move opposed by Campbell-Bannerman himself, who argued that it was quite wrong to 'interpose another circle of authority between the Shadow Cabinet and the back benches' (Jenkins, 1965, 108).

Balfour and the Conservative Party

The Conservative Government and, after 1905, Opposition, was split over Tariff Reform and Colonial Preference with a difference of opinion between the Prime Minister, Balfour, who had succeeded Salisbury in 1902, and Joseph Chamberlain. Considerable quantities of correspondence flowed between the two men on the issues which divided them, Balfour soon looking into the question of providing the party with a common policy, particularly on fiscal matters. In February 1906 he met Mr and Mrs Joseph Chamberlain and Austen Chamberlain, though nothing definite was agreed upon on this occasion (Dugdale, 15). There was also a meeting early in 1906 of the Conservative leaders at Balfour's house in Carlton House Gardens in order to examine the reasons for their defeat in the election but, evidently, no common agreement was reached (Chamberlain, 37). At this time Joseph Chamberlain was acting as the temporary Leader of the Opposition; Balfour had lost his seat in the election, later being returned for the City of London and taking his seat early in March 1906.

Despite the fact that the Conservatives had suffered a most severe defeat and were quite deeply divided over Tariff Reform and Colonial Preference, Blanche Dugdale can still assert, somewhat surprisingly, that the Opposition was in good fighting order. The Opposition may have experienced the 'joys of battle', but there were, nevertheless, rumblings of discontent from the Conservative backbenches over the lack of a party programme. The dis-

28

satisfaction even spread to some members of the Shadow Cabinet. Party divisions and controversy continued throughout 1907 and 1908, in fact right up to the outbreak of the First World War. Sir Austen Chamberlain, in a letter written on 12 February 1907, refers to a difficult meeting of the Shadow Cabinet at which the only support he received appeared to be that of Linlithgow, 'if I did not mistake his becks and nods and wreathed smiles' (Chamberlain, 50). At a meeting the following day, Chamberlain reported to the Tariff Reformers what had gone on in the Shadow Cabinet, stating that his view had been an isolated one amongst members of the 'ex-Cabinet'. The Shadow Cabinet met again at 6.30 p.m. the same evening and, evidently, Chamberlain was asked to disclose all that had been said at the Tariff Reform meeting, though pledged to secrecy. In the event, the Shadow Cabinet agreed to Chamberlain's pressure for the amendments proposed by the Tariff Reformers at their earlier meeting with Chamberlain. The Tariff Reform issue was still troubling the Shadow Cabinet in 1909, Chamberlain attending a meeting on 17 February, together with Balfour, Chaplin, Wyndham and Londonderry at which the Tariff Reformers appear to have got their own way (Chamberlain, 144-5).

Sir Austen Chamberlain also refers to the Shadow Cabinet in 1910, stating clearly that this had become the accepted title used at this time. The meeting in question was one at which the Conservative leaders discussed whether constitutional experts from the United States, Canada and Australia should be invited to give evidence to the Constitutional Conference which was attempting to settle the question of the powers of the House of Lords. The Conservative Shadow Cabinet met at Lansdowne House and was attended by some twenty party leaders including Balfour, Halsbury, Cawdor, Lansdowne, A. Chamberlain, Selborne, Long, Finlay, Carson, Lyttleton and Akers-Douglas (Chamberlain, 295-96).

The Conservatives and the 1911 Crisis

The Conservatives had rejected the 1909 Lloyd George Budget by virtue of their large majority in the House of Lords and, of course, this caused tremendous controversy about the powers of the Second Chamber, controversy which had been greatly complicated by the death of Edward VII and the accession of George V. The desire of both major parties not to confront the new King with such a serious constitutional crisis had, therefore, led to the setting up of the Constitutional Conference consisting of four leaders from each party, the intention being to reach some settlement, but this did not happen.

The controversy led to the holding of two General Elections during 1910, the first in January necessitated by the Lords' rejection of the Budget resulting in a gain of some 100 seats by the Conservatives. The second, held in December, resulted in a dead-heat, the two major parties winning 272 seats each, thus leaving the Conservatives in the role of His Majesty's Opposition. Further meetings of the Conservative Shadow Cabinet were held during March and July 1911 at Carlton Gardens amidst considerable disunity, particularly the July meetings. The cause of the trouble was the Prime Minister's secret arrangement with George V prior to the December election to create sufficient Liberal Peers to enable the passage of a Parliament Bill to curtail the powers of the Second Chamber provided that the Liberals won the election.

Balfour was very indignant indeed when he learnt, in July 1911, of the arrangement between Asquith and the King, indignation based not so much upon surprise at what had happened, since he had anticipated just such a move in January 1910, as at the delay in being notified of the situation (Chamberlain, 196-200). The Leader of the Opposition immediately called a meeting of the Shadow Cabinet for 7 July 1911, at which there was a sharp division of opinion as to the tactics to be adopted; there followed a second meeting on 21 July, which split into those in favour of submitting to Asquith's threat and the passing of the Parliament Bill, and those who were determined to oppose any such move. There were twenty-two people present at this second meeting, those for resistance being Selborne, Halsbury, Salisbury, A. Chamberlain, Wyndham, Carson, F. E. Smith and Balcarres, those for capitulation being the leader, Balfour, Lansdowne, Curzon, Midleton, Londonderry, Bonar Law, Akers-Douglas, Lyttelton, Chaplin, Long, Derby, Ashborne, Steel-Maitland and Finlay (Dugdale, 49).

Correspondence passed between Balfour and Austen Chamberlain following this very serious schism in the Opposition ranks. Balfour considered that Chamberlain underrated the difficulties faced by the leader, the 'Shadow Cabinet showing irreconcilable differences of opinion'. In Balfour's opinion, 'had it been a real Cabinet, one of two things would have followed . . . either the dissentient minority would have resigned, or they would have silently acquiesced in the decision of the majority'. The Leader of the Opposition continued that there could be no question of resignation in the case of a Shadow Cabinet, a somewhat strange pronouncement (Chamberlain, 350-1). Balfour was very upset by the apparent lack of self-discipline and the absence of any principle of collective responsibility in his Shadow Cabinet, resigning the leadership some three months after the meeting of 21 July, to be succeeded by Andrew Bonar Law.

Before going on to consider the remaining years up to the beginning of the First World War, it is necessary to pause for a moment longer on the period of Balfour's leadership of Opposition. It appears that there were no definite rules as to who should be summoned to meetings of the Conservative Shadow Cabinet. H. Chaplin continued to be invited though he had left the Government before the 1903 reconstruction, whilst F. E. Smith had never served in a Ministry. The ex-law officers were usually present as were Balcarres and Steel-Maitland, the Chief Whip and Party Organizer (Dugdale, 49-50).

Further developments up to 1918

Bonar Law held a number of meetings during the early part of 1912, together with Lansdowne, Selborne, Curzon, Long and Austen Chamberlain to discuss parliamentary tactics. There was also a meeting of the Shadow Cabinet late in 1912 attended by Bonar Law, Chamberlain, Chaplin, Lansdowne, Londonderry, Derby, Long, Selborne, Wyndham, Balcarres, Lyttelton, Finlay and Steel-Maitland which Chamberlain described as the 'best meeting of its kind that I have ever attended'. In his biography of Bonar Law, Robert Blake gives a fascinating insight into the delicacies of party management and diplomacy. The incident in question was Bonar Law's first eve of Session dinner for Opposition leaders in February 1912. Balcarres, the Chief Whip, provided Bonar Law with a long list of do's and dont's concerning etiquette and procedure. It seems that a good deal of importance was attached not only to who was invited to attend, but also to where persons sat in relation to the Leader of the Opposition. Balcarres made the point that 'all this was a tiresome detail of dinner party precedence, but it none the less connotes the future complexion of ministries' (Blake, 1955, 102).

Those members of the Shadow Cabinet in the House of Lords were summoned by Lansdowne, those in the Commons by Bonar Law. Evidently, the exact rules as to who should be summoned were anything but clear, there being 'no particular qualification and no definite membership'. Balcarres provided a list of nineteen persons usually summoned to attend, which comprised Lansdowne, Halsbury, Ashborne, Londonderry, Chilston (Akers-Douglas), Selborne, Derby, Midleton, Curzon, Salisbury, Balfour, A. Chamberlain, Lyttelton, Long, Wyndham, F. E. Smith, Finlay, Carson and Chaplin (Blake, 1955, 103). Apparently the Shadow Cabinet gave considerable trouble to the leaders. Failing to invite certain persons caused offence and ill-feeling, whilst those who were invited regarded themselves almost as certainties for inclusion in a future Cabinet, which was not always the case. A meeting was called in February 1912 which included what was described as 'eleven House of Commons Shadows'. Approaching Bonar Law, Lansdowne made the point that if eleven were to be included from the Commons, then Londonderry, and perhaps also Halsbury, should be included from the Upper House (Blake, 1955, 103-8).

Robert Blake states that difficulties like this were quite common and therefore Bonar Law and Lansdowne called meetings of the Shadow Cabinet as infrequently as possible, restricting them to matters of great importance. This situation has parallels with that which existed during the second half of the nineteenth century, when Shadow Cabinets were called only at times of crisis or prior to Sessions of Parliament.

Further meetings of the Shadow Cabinet were held between 1912 and 1914 until, with the onset of war, the first Coalition Government was formed in May 1915, with Asquith as Prime Minister. Bonar Law, Lansdowne, A. Chamberlain, Long, F. E. Smith, Carson, Selborne, Balfour and Curzon were all included in the Asquith Cabinet, Chaplin apparently acting as a 'nominal leader of the Opposition' (Oxford and Asquith, i, 177). This government was succeeded in December 1916 by a second Coalition Government, this time with Lloyd George as Prime Minister. Asquith remained completely outside the new administration, offering criticism where necessary, but in the main, supporting the Government in its conduct of the war.

The period from 1880 to the First World War provided a period of steady development in the history of the Shadow Cabinet. The term 'Shadow Cabinet' progressively replaced its older counterpart 'late Cabinet' in the vocabulary of Opposition, being used alike by both politicians and commentators. However, some statesmen like Balfour and Bonar Law still harboured certain reservations as to the necessity for the existence of such a body. We have also seen that collective unity and discipline was not a marked feature of the Shadow Cabinet at this time. The main difference between this and earlier periods appears to have been the greater use made of this body by the Opposition and also the increased numbers of persons invited to attend.

4
Elected front bench

For the first time in British political history, the General Election held on Wednesday, 14 November 1922, produced an official Labour Opposition in Parliament. The long established 'balance of power' between the Conservative and Liberal parties had been broken. For decades, office had alternated between these two great and traditional parties, the First World War finally bringing some of the leaders together in a Coalition led by Asquith and from 1916 by Lloyd George. However from 1922 onwards the Labour Party steadily consolidated its position as the second party in the state and thereby relegated a divided Liberal Party to the comparative insignificance of a third party in the House of Commons. The Election itself produced few surprises. The Conservatives, who had in any case dominated the Coalition, secured 345 seats, the Labour Party 142 seats and the Liberals 116, divided between the supporters of Asquith and Lloyd George.

Emergence of a Labour Opposition in 1922

The Labour Party quickly set about adapting itself to undertake the duties and responsibilities of His Majesty's Opposition. The Front Benches of both its rivals were appointed at the discretion of the respective party leaders, though they invariably contained a high proportion of ex-Ministers. However, the Labour Opposition possessed only a handful of men with any experience of office at all and then in wartime Coalition Governments. Much of the organization was carried out by a so called 'Big Five' which consisted of Ramsay MacDonald, Snowden, Henderson, Thomas and Clynes. Apparently, it was these five men who planned the shape and composition of the first Labour Government in 1924 (McHenry, 140).

It is wrong to assume that the Party in Parliament (P.L.P.) was devoid of all normal trappings of a Parliamentary Opposition. From 1906 onwards, the P.L.P., then some forty strong, had annually elected its principal officers and held meetings to discuss tactics and select speakers for debates, the Party following the practice of selecting one speaker to represent the official views of the party in all important debates (McKenzie, 391). Evidently, at the beginning of each Session the P.L.P. reviewed the various annual Conference resolutions in order to build up a programme of legislative measures which they attempted to bring to the notice of the Government. If individual Labour Members of Parliament were lucky enough in the ballot for the introduction of Private Members' Bills, it was agreed that the Member concerned would 'adopt' one of the prior agreed party topics (Bromhead, 50-1 and 112-16). However, there was no Shadow Cabinet in the usual sense of the expression to direct and co-ordinate the work of the party in Parliament. There was no possibility of creating any kind of 'late Cabinet'. On the other hand, it was quite conceivable that a Committee consisting of Members of Parliament could perform similar functions to those exercised by a traditional Shadow Cabinet. This is, in fact, what happened, the P.L.P. adopting a Shadow Cabinet system based upon the elective principle. It consisted of the Leader and Deputy Leader of the P.L.P. the Chief Whip in the House of Commons and an elected 'Parliamentary Executive Committee' (P.E.C.) of twelve members with

36

seats in the House of Commons. It was not until 1925 that
Labour Peers were invited to take part in meetings of the
Shadow Cabinet and P.L.P. as a whole. The first Labour
Shadow Cabinet, constituted following the election of the
Parliamentary Executive Committee in February 1923,
included the following fifteen persons:

J. R. MacDonald
(Leader)

J. Clynes
(Deputy Leader)

A. Henderson
(Chief Whip)

W. Adamson	T. Shaw
R. Davies	E. Shinwell
T. Johnston	P. Snowden
F. Jowett	J. Thomas
G. Lansbury	S. Webb
E. Morel	J. Wheatley

J. Ramsay MacDonald had been elected Leader of the
P.L.P., and thus of the Opposition, at a full meeting of the
party held some eight days after the Election, on 22
November 1922. The emergence of the Labour Party as
'His Majesty's Opposition' led to a certain amount of confusion and misunderstanding as to who was entitled to
sit on the Opposition Front Bench in the House of Commons. The Speaker proposed that the Labour Party should
be given preference over the Liberals in all important
debates and on the majority of Supply Days, but that the
Liberals should, as a concession, occupy the greater part
of the Opposition Front Bench. This suggestion annoyed
the more militant members of the Labour Party, who insisted that the seats should be occupied by their own
leaders.

The majority of the Parliamentary Executive Committee
elected in February 1923 served in the 1924 MacDonald
administration. Adamson, Jowett, Shaw, Snowden,

Thomas, Webb and Wheatley were given Cabinet posts, whilst Davies and Shinwell became Junior Ministers. The Opposition Bench was given such little time to accustom itself to its duties, before being called upon to form an administration, that no clear relationship between Opposition responsibilities and subsequent Government offices could really be seen. However, it appears that Wheatley was recognized in the House as an expert on housing, moving the official Opposition rejection of Neville Chamberlain's Housing Bill on 24 April 1923 (H.C. Debates, Vol. 163, col. 325). Another Front Bencher, T. Johnston became a specialist on Colonial affairs during 1923, though he was not given any position in the 1924 Government, having handled rather badly an attack upon the Conservative Government over the question of the affairs of a company growing cotton in the Sudan (Middlemas, 127). MacDonald, Clynes, Henderson and Jowett spoke on a wide range of topics. Of the other Opposition Front Bench spokesmen, Adamson, who became Secretary for Scotland in the 1924 Cabinet, contributed to the Second Reading of the Education (Scotland) Bill, Shaw, appointed to the Ministry of Labour, spoke on the Workman's Compensation (No. 2) Bill and Shinwell, who was made responsible for the Mines Department at the Board of Trade, spoke quite often on the coal industry. Snowden, soon to become Chancellor of the Exchequer, made contributions to debates on income tax, the Budget proposals and the Finance Bill (H.C. Debates, Vols. 162-5, 1923).

The Leader of the Opposition was called upon to form Labour's first Government in January 1924, following Baldwin's decision to ask the King for a dissolution of Parliament in November 1923. The new Prime Minister, who had succeeded Bonar Law in May 1923, was convinced that in order to fight unemployment, it was necessary to reintroduce Protection. The Election held on 6 December 1923, resulted in a loss of over ninety Conservative seats. The Labour Opposition with 191 increased its strength in the House of Commons by fifty seats. On 21 January 1924, the Conservative Government was defeated by seventy-two votes and the following day George V sent for Ramsay MacDonald. The composition of the Cabinet of twenty persons was divided equally between members of the P.E.C. elected in February 1923 and non-Committee members such as Parmoor, Haldane, Chelmsford, Buxton, Walsh and Wedgwood. However, as is well known, the life of MacDonald's first administration was due to be very brief indeed, the Conservatives returning to office in November 1924.

Following their return to Opposition, the P.L.P. elected, in December, its second P.E.C. The new Committee contained only four of the men elected in February 1923, namely Lansbury, who topped the poll, Snowden, who came third, Thomas, who finished fourth and Wheatley, who took fifth place. The newly elected members of the Committee were Graham, Henderson, Lees-Smith, Maxton, Roberts, Smillie, who took second place in the poll, Trevelyan and Wedgwood. Ben Spoor took over as Chief Whip in place of Arthur Henderson, whilst MacDonald and Clynes retained their posts as Leader and Deputy Leader. Trevelyan and Wedgwood had both been members of the 1924 MacDonald Cabinet, Trevelyan at the Board of Education and Wedgwood the Duchy of Lancaster, whilst Roberts had been Minister of Pensions outside the Cabinet.

The P.L.P. held similar elections for the P.E.C. in December 1925, 1926 and 1927, although there appears to have been no election in 1928. From 1925 onwards the degree of stability and continuity of membership was more marked, seven of the Committee elected in December 1924 holding their places in 1925, whilst ten of the 1925 Committee were re-elected in 1926 and 1927. Six men, Graham, Lansbury, Lees-Smith, Snowden, Thomas and Trevelyan held their places on the Committee continuously between December 1924 and December 1928. Adamson, the ex-Secretary for Scotland, who had failed to retain his place on the P.E.C. when it was re-elected in 1924, continued, nevertheless, to be a principal spokesman on Scottish matters, taking part in debates between December 1924 and December 1925 on Scottish agriculture, education and numerous other matters. He regained his place on the Committee in 1925.

Relations between the P.L.P. and the I.L.P.

The Independent Labour Party had been established in 1893 and was one of the founding members of the Labour Party. Whilst I.L.P. members were, in the main, simply orthodox members of the P.L.P., the Party continued to hold its own Conferences and sponsor its own parliamentary candidates. For ten years the I.L.P. provided some of the most stringent criticism of the P.L.P., finally being disaffiliated by the 1932 Labour Party Conference. Some of the leading members of the P.L.P., including MacDonald, were also members of the I.L.P. Where did their allegiance lie? Some put the I.L.P. first, but the majority apparently supported the larger P.L.P. on most issues (Dowse, 41). According to Dowse, when the P.L.P. first became the official Opposition in 1922, its relations with the I.L.P. worsened, though the latter continued to wield considerable influence over the Labour Party as a whole.

MacDonald's responsible approach to the duties of an Opposition Leader in the House of Commons did not please the more militant elements within the ranks of the I.L.P. and led to a certain tension. There was at least one definite revolt against the 'parliamentary approach' during a debate on the Scottish Estimates in June 1923, when five members of the I.L.P., Maxton, Wheatley, Stephen, Shinwell and Buchanan incurred the displeasure of the Chair by their unseemly behaviour and were suspended after MacDonald's attempts to get those involved to temper their language had failed (Dowse, 93-4). The suspended M.P.s were summoned to appear before the Shadow Cabinet on 3 July, but they still refused to withdraw. It was finally decided that the P.L.P. issue a short statement of rebuke and no more. The suspension was withdrawn late in July and the members apparently returned triumphantly to the House of Commons (Middlemas, 131). The incident was serious in that the rebels included two members of the Shadow Cabinet elected in February 1923, Wheatley and Shinwell, the former consistently putting allegiance to the I.L.P. over that given to the P.L.P. (Dowse, 96).

Following the defeat of the Labour Party in 1924, the I.L.P. was critical of the P.L.P., and attempts were apparently made to remove MacDonald from the leadership. The 'rebels' also proposed to model themselves along 'Parnellite' lines, opposing the Baldwin Government vigorously, 'whatever the rest of the P.L.P. decided' (Dowse, 118-19). Lansbury, Maxton, Wheatley, Wedgwood and Kirkwood also determined not to stand for election to the Shadow Cabinet. In the event, following the intervention of Henderson, only Maxton actually carried out his threat. Of the others, only Lansbury retained his place on the P.E.C., slipping from first to tenth place in the poll (*The Times*, 5 December 1925). The I.L.P. members constantly pressed for more vigorous Opposition from MacDonald but without very much success. From about 1925 onwards, the division between the I.L.P. and the P.L.P. became marked, 'middle class elements like Buxton, Trevelyan and Attlee transferring from the I.L.P. to their Divisional Labour Parties . . .' (Dowse, 124).

Lloyd George and the Liberal Shadow Cabinet

The Liberals were clearly a poor third in the 1924 General Election. However, they appear to have possessed a 'Shadow Cabinet' which was known as such. On the day that the General Strike broke out, 3 May 1926, there was a meeting of this body attended by both Asquith (Lord Oxford) and Lloyd George. A further meeting was called for by the Chief Whip on 10 May, the only notable absentee being Lloyd George. The Liberal Shadow Cabinet apparently agreed to support the Government but to press for a resumption of negotiations between the Government and the Trades Union Council (T.U.C.).

Lloyd George's absence annoyed Asquith, who felt this to be as serious as a Cabinet Minister failing to attend a Cabinet meeting, a course which usually culminated in the resignation of the Minister concerned. Lloyd George further aggravated the situation by writing an article on the issue for the United Press. Asquith rebuked Lloyd George and declared that he had resigned from the Shadow Cabinet. On 1 June, Asquith received a letter from twelve of his Shadow Cabinet colleagues supporting the action he had taken. The letter, which contained the signatures of Grey (of Fallodon), Simon, Runciman, Lincolnshire, Buckmaster, Buxton, Maclean, Cowdray, Phillipps, Howard, Pringle and Collins was also sent to, and published by, *The Times*. According to *The Times*, of the twelve signatories all but Lord Lincolnshire were members of the Shadow Cabinet. Six members of the Shadow Cabinet did not sign the letter, four of them, Beauchamp, McCurdy, Macnamara and Masterman being regarded as supporters of Lloyd George; the remaining two were Macpherson and Wedgwood Benn. Lloyd George did not consider his absence from the Shadow Cabinet meeting to be of great moment. In a speech to the Manchester Reform Club on 4 June 1926, he insisted that he had been deliberately excommunicated from the inner ranks of the Liberal Opposition and spoke scornfully of the 'privilege of being a Liberal Shadow' (Spender & Asquith, ii, 367).

Asquith and Lloyd George appear to have been quite widely divided over the necessity for, and effectiveness of, a Liberal Shadow Cabinet. In a letter to Sir Godfrey Collins, Asquith states quite clearly that the 'Shadow Cabinet is the substitute when the leaders of a party are in opposition for the actual Cabinet when they are in office, and it has always been understood that membership of it involves similar obligations' (*The Times*, 2 June 1962). It is not surprising, therefore, that when Lloyd George succeeded Asquith as leader in October 1926, meetings of the Liberal Shadow Cabinet do not appear to have been convened. Indeed, it has even been suggested that the Liberals discarded the idea completely after 1926 (Mowat, 348).

Amery, Churchill and the Conservative Shadow Cabinet

Between 1929 and 1931, as indeed during the short interlude in 1924, the Conservative Opposition possessed a Shadow Cabinet.

Birkenhead, as the ex-Secretary of State for India, took a prominent part in the Shadow Cabinet deliberations over the Statute of Westminster, the Simon Commission and the future of India, including one such meeting which was held in an 'uncomfortable room in the Conservative offices in Palace Chambers' (Birkenhead, 521).

The years between 1929 and 1931 were uneasy ones for Baldwin. There was much restlessness amongst the ranks of the Conservatives with his leadership. It appears that following the 1929 election defeat, there were almost instant discussions between Lloyd George, Austen Chamberlain and Churchill aimed at forming an 'anti-socialist coalition' to turn out MacDonald. Leo Amery did not agree with this development and said so during a speech on Empire Trade on 9 July 1929. Two days later an 'animated Shadow Cabinet discussion' was held on the issue, though no definite decision seems to have have emerged (Amery, ii, 508-11). Amery was later dropped from the inner councils of the Party over the question of Preference and his support for the 'Empire Crusade' staged by the Beaverbrook and Rothermere Press. Amery was invited back into the Shadow Cabinet, or 'Business Committee' as it was known at this time, early in 1931. It was now Churchill's turn to remove

43

himself from the Conservative Opposition hierarchy in
Parliament. He was particularly aggrieved by the official
attitude of both his own Party and the Government over
the question of Indian self-rule. He expressed his sentiments
upon this matter clearly and unequivocably in a number
of speeches and articles. The climax came in January 1931.
During the debate following the Prime Minister's statement on the Round Table Conference concerning India,
Churchill made it clear that the opinions he was expressing
were personal. He was speaking neither for the official
Opposition, nor for the Leader of the Opposition. This, com-
ing from a senior member of the Shadow Cabinet clearly
foreshadowed trouble. The following day, Churchill
wrote to his Leader stating that in view of their diver-
gence of opinion over India, it would be better for him
not to attend future meetings of the Business Committee.
Baldwin, in his reply dated 28 January, regretted Churchill's
decision but agreed that it was correct in the circumstances.
The Times stated that Churchill would continue to sit on
the Opposition Front Bench but not take any part in direct-
ing the policy of the Opposition. The article went on to say
that the Shadow Cabinet had been abolished some time ago
and its place taken by the Business Committee which
'meets from time to time to consider the work which the
House of Commons is asked to transact'. The Committee
apparently consisted of, for the most part, ex-Ministers,
but Baldwin was entitled to invite any member of the
Party to its deliberations (*The Times*, 30 January 1931).
This final statement is most interesting. Was there a
Shadow Cabinet in existence or not? Amery refers to meetings of the Shadow Cabinet as does Duff Cooper (Viscount
Norwich). According to Lord Templewood, the Shadow
Cabinet had not met since October 1929. In its stead there
were 'frequent meetings of a small business committee to
which Baldwin invited Chamberlain, Churchill, Hailsham,
Peel, Oliver, Stanley and myself' (Templewood, 48). This
means that during this period the affairs of the Conserva-

44

tive Opposition were controlled by the six or seven members of what can only be described as an 'inner' Shadow
Cabinet, together with any other persons Baldwin wished
to invite.

5
From MacDonald to Churchill

The 1931 General Election witnessed the temporary disintegration of the Labour Party. Following the financial and political crisis in July that year, resulting in the resignation of nine members of his Cabinet and the subsequent downfall of the Government, MacDonald accepted the King's invitation to become head of a 'National' Government. His decision to accept taken, apparently, without consulting the Labour Party beforehand, proved unacceptable to the majority of its members. At a joint meeting of the T.U.C. General Council, the National Executive Committee and the Consultative Committee of the P.L.P. on 26 August 1931, support was expressed for the stand taken by the nine former Cabinet Ministers and the meeting recommended that the P.L.P. constitute itself as the official Parliamentary Opposition (Bassett, 183). Two days later, this decision was endorsed by a full meeting of the P.L.P. and Henderson was elected Leader with Clynes and Graham as joint Deputy Leaders.

When the Election was held, on 27 October, the 'National' Government led by MacDonald secured an overwhelming victory with 554 seats to the Labour Party's 52 seats. The resulting situation in Parliament was one in which the Opposition seemed almost doomed to extinction, so great had become the imbalance of parties. However,

the Opposition not only survived but actually contrived
to function in quite an efficient manner.

Lansbury becomes Leader

Arthur Henderson, who had lost his seat in Parliament
at the 1931 Election, resigned from the Leadership in
October 1932. His successor, Lansbury, was the only former
Cabinet Minister who did survive the Election and was
therefore an obvious choice to lead the Opposition in the
House of Commons. His Deputy was Clement Attlee. The
Opposition was of ridiculously small proportions. Nevertheless the P.L.P. quickly established a recognizable, though
diminished Shadow Cabinet and Front Bench which consisted of Lansbury, Attlee, Edwards (Chief Whip) and an
elected Parliamentary Committee reduced, temporarily, to
seven. The elected members were, Cripps, Grenfell, Hicks,
Jones, Lunn, Maclean and Williams. These seven men retained their places in the Labour Shadow Cabinet from
November 1931 until 1935.

Apart from Lansbury, Attlee and Cripps, the Opposition
Front Bench lacked ministerial experience, but, nevertheless, adapted to their new responsibilities with commend-
able ease. Everybody worked very hard during this period
since most of them had previously concerned themselves
with one area or subject at the most, but now members
had to be prepared to speak on a wide variety of subjects.
Tom Williams, an ex-miner, was particularly good on
agriculture, whilst Lansbury, Cripps and Attlee worked
very closely together, one of them always being present
on the Opposition Front Bench when the House was sitting
(Attlee, 76-7). In addition, the Shadow Cabinet met every
day before Question Time to settle plans for the day and
the P.L.P. met at least once every week. The Opposition
in the House of Lords was directed by the Leader of the
Labour Peers, Ponsonby, the Peers' Chief Whip, Marley and
also by Lords Buxton, Sanderson and Snell, joined later

47

by Addison, Listowel and Strabolgi (McHenry, 176).

The Opposition made considerable gains at the 1935 Election, returning some 154 Members and the I.L.P., 4 Members. This corrected to some extent the imbalance between Government and Opposition, the P.L.P. once more electing a full twelve members to the Parliamentary Executive Committee in November 1935. Lansbury had injured himself in a fall towards the end of 1933, resulting in an absence of nine months. During this period, Attlee acted as Leader, Lansbury finally resigning in 1935. Attlee now took over as Leader with Greenwood as Deputy Leader. With the increasing threat to world peace from both Germany and Italy, Lansbury had found it increasingly difficult to reconcile his pacifist opinions with those of his colleagues. At the Labour Party Conference at Brighton in the Autumn of 1935, the aged Leader attempted to explain his position to the delegates. However, following a most powerful and destructive speech from Bevin, the Conference voted overwhelmingly in favour of Dalton's resolution calling for sanctions against Mussolini. Lansbury resigned some few days later.

An elected Shadow Cabinet and Front Bench

Between 1935 and 1939 the Labour Opposition, though increased in size and strengthened by the return of some of its senior members, was still heavily outnumbered by the Government. However, Attlee appears to have led his troops efficiently subjecting the Government to 'continual and searching criticism' and at the same time putting forward a 'coherent and constructive alternative policy' (Jenkins, 170).

When the results of the ballot for the Shadow Cabinet were announced in November 1935, five of those who had served so consistently and well since 1931 were re-elected, namely Grenfell, Jones, Lunn, Maclean and Williams. Cripps, on the other hand, appears to have retired from the Front Bench, joining his old leader, Lansbury, on the third bench below the gangway on the Opposition side of the House (Cooke, 177). The remaining seven places on the Committee were filled by Alexander, Clynes (who topped the poll), Dalton, Johnston, Lees-Smith, Morrison and Pethick-Lawrence, Shinwell returning in November 1937. Of the others, Johnston and Jones were re-elected up to November 1939, whilst Lunn and Maclean ceased to be included. Clynes, who had been both Chairman and Deputy Leader of the P.L.P. was *elected* to serve on the Committee twice, in November 1935 and again the following year. However, it is interesting to note that during the Session 1937-8, Clynes, Cripps and ten other persons were elected to sit on the Opposition Front Bench. This new development appears to have been introduced in order to eliminate the custom whereby ex-Ministers sat on the Opposition Front Benches, as of right. The ten persons elected in addition to Clynes and Cripps were Lawson, Hall, Davies, Wedgwood, Montague, Ammon, Roberts, Westwood, Kennedy and Parkinson (1938 Labour Party Conference Report). The 1939 Conference Report also refers to the election of such a body of men who were 'elected to sit with the Officers and Executive on the Front Bench', the only change being the replacement of Westwood by J. Griffiths. The inclusion of these men on the Front Bench meant that its ranks were considerably swelled, constituting what appears to have been almost a second Parliamentary Executive Committee. This new group included experienced former Ministers and its members made regular and often lengthy contributions to debates from the Front Bench. Two of them, Hall and Lawson, 'graduated' to full Shadow Cabinet membership in November 1939. Surprisingly, there appears to be very little evidence about the existence of this group of elected Front Benchers other than in the 1938 and 1939 Labour Party Conference Reports, and even these fail to describe how and by whom these twelve members were elected, but presumably it was by a ballot amongst the members of the P.L.P.

The Labour Opposition and the Second World War

Following Neville Chamberlain's announcement of Britain's declaration of war against Germany on 3 September 1939, the Labour Party Shadow Cabinet and National Executive meeting in joint session, declined to participate in the Government. They did, however, issue a joint statement supporting the action of the British and French Governments. The 1940 invasion of Norway and Denmark led to a Labour vote of censure on the Government whose majority fell from a possible 247 to a mere 81 votes. Chamberlain apparently invited Attlee and Greenwood to take part in a reconstruction of the Government, Attlee reporting the conversation to the Shadow Cabinet before informing Chamberlain that they would not serve with him as Prime Minister. With the replacement of Chamberlain by Churchill in May 1940, the Labour Party agreed to enter the wartime Coalition Government, Attlee, Bevin, Cripps, Greenwood and Morrison all holding Cabinet offices at some stage between 1940 and 1945.

With the outbreak of war, party differences were for the most part buried, though the Labour Party still constituted 'His Majesty's Opposition'. Shortly after the leading members of the Opposition had joined the Government, the P.L.P. elected an Administrative Committee which occupied the Opposition Front Bench and acted as an Executive Committee with an elected Chairman standing in during Attlee's absence. Apparently, until his death in 1941, Lees-Smith put the 'Business Question' on Thursdays and discharged the formal duties normally associated with the Leader of the Opposition. The Administrative Committee included those members of the Shadow Cabinet who did not enter the wartime Government, together with other members who were entitled to sit on the Front Bench.

Labour Ministers, who were also members of the Shadow Cabinet, were afforded *ex officio* status.

Victory yet defeat

The decision of the British electorate in 1945 came as a shock to many people, not least the massed ranks of the Conservative Party. When the result of the Election was finally announced on 26 July Winston Churchill, the victor in war, had been decisively beaten at the polls. The Labour Party, led by Clement Attlee, won 393 seats, a majority of 180 over the broken and bewildered ranks of the Conservative Party. Lord Kilmuir described the Conservative defeat as a 'cataclysm', a sudden catastrophic defeat in which some five former Cabinet Ministers and twenty-six Junior Ministers had lost their seats in Parliament. Churchill had apparently hoped that the wartime Coalition might remain in existence long enough to tackle the immense problems facing the nation in the immediate post-war period. The majority of his colleagues, on the other hand, were in favour of an early General Election. Churchill thus resigned in May, being invited almost immediately to form another Government as leader of the largest party in the state. The new Government, which soon became known as the 'Caretaker' Government, was composed primarily of Conservatives and National Liberals, but included a number of non-party former Coalition Ministers such as Sir John Anderson and Sir Andrew Duncan.

Churchill as Leader of the Opposition

Once the Election post-mortems had been concluded, the Conservatives turned their attention towards reconstructing the Party machine, the greater part of which had fallen into disuse during the war. The remnants of the Party in Parliament had also to prepare for the relatively unaccustomed role of 'His Majesty's Opposition'. In September 1945, Conservative Central Office announced details of the Party's plans for organizing its forces in Parliament into a 'united and virile Opposition'. There was to be a Shadow Cabinet, a Standing Conference of Committees and close liaison between the Front and back benches through the extensive use of specialist committees. The Standing Conference of Committees was the precursor of the Business Committee. It met just before the Shadow Cabinet under Eden and made recommendations to the Shadow Cabinet about future parliamentary business.

Although the Opposition was inexperienced and badly outnumbered in the House of Commons, it possessed a potentially very powerful Shadow Cabinet team whose members collectively laid claim to a considerable pool of parliamentary and Cabinet experience. Winston Churchill was supported by, amongst others, Eden, Salisbury, Stanley, Lyttelton, Butler, Macmillan, Stuart, Winterton, Morrison, Elliot, Assheton, Crookshank, Swinton, Maxwell Fyfe (Kilmuir), Woolton, Anderson, Hudson, Law, Peake, Lennox-Boyd, Bracken, Dugdale, Manningham-Buller, Sandys, Thorneycroft, Miss Horsburgh and Reid. The Shadow Cabinet met every Wednesday evening at 6 p.m., supplemented by a fortnightly lunch at the Savoy Hotel (Kilmuir, 148-9). Lord Salisbury was Leader of the Opposition in the House of Lords, whilst J. Stuart was the Opposition Chief Whip in the House of Commons (succeeded in 1948 by P. Buchan-Hepburn). Contrary to the practice of the Labour Party, the Conservative Peers' Chief Whip, Lord Fortescue, does not appear to have attended meetings of the Shadow Cabinet as of right, but may well have been invited to do so on certain occasions.

The Conservative Opposition took quite some time to adjust itself to its new surroundings, whilst Churchill's early record as Leader of the Opposition gave rise to certain misgivings amongst his colleagues. Churchill, by his own admission, was deeply distressed at the prospect of sinking from a national to a party leader, a feeling which may

well have affected both his own performance and also
that of his colleagues. He may have been suffering, also,
from a reaction following his supreme effort during the
war years. Evidently, he was often absent from the House
as, for example during the Second Reading of the Bank
of England Bill on 29 October, when it was left to Sir John
Anderson and Oliver Stanley to put the Opposition case
(Hoffman, 228). In the House, much of the day-to-day work
of leading the Opposition appears to have been undertaken
by Anthony Eden, 'Churchill making his memorable contributions on the great occasions' (Broad, 1955). The Leader
of the Opposition was not alone in the practice of absen-
teeism, 'Rab' Butler having also been absent during the
Second Reading of the Bank of England Bill. Eden was
absent during the announcement, by Herbert Morrison
on 19 November 1945, that the Government intended
to nationalize electricity, gas and transport. In fact, it
appears that of the Front Bench, only Stanley and Lyttelton were present in the House at the time. The outcome
was an immediate meeting of the 1922 Committee at
which a number of promises were made, including one
that, in future, either Churchill or Eden would be in the
House for all major debates (Hoffman, 229).

Opposition becomes more effective

The Government's extensive plans for public ownership
consumed a considerable amount of parliamentary time,
members of the Shadow Cabinet being well to the fore
in all subsequent debates in the Chamber. Most of the leading spokesmen had to make a speech in the House once
a fortnight and if they were 'shadowing' a particular Department, they were expected to speak very frequently.
It appears to have been general practice for members of
the Shadow Cabinet to be given responsibility for leading
the Opposition case on a specific Bill during its passage
through the House of Commons. Oliver Stanley was concerned with financial debates, Robert Hudson with

agricultural matters, whilst Oliver Lyttelton was 'charged with leading the Opposition to the Bill nationalizing Steel' (Chandos, 336). During debates, the opening and closing Opposition speeches were the responsibility of the Front Benchers concerned. The Second Reading of the Coal Industry Nationalization Bill on 29 January 1946, was opened for the Opposition by Eden and closed by Macmillan who, as Chairman of the Conservative Fuel and Power Committee, also opened the Supply debate on the Coal situation on 24 July (H.C. Debates, Vols. 418 & 426).

Osbert Peake seems to have been responsible for National Insurance, playing a prominent role in debates on this subject. He was also Chairman of the Conservative Home Office and Welfare Committee between 1945 and 1950. The National Insurance Bill was, in fact, given an unopposed Second and Third Reading, but not so the National Health Service Bill. During the Second Reading on 30 April 1946, the opening speech for the Opposition was made by Richard Law and the closing speech by J. Reid, whilst the Third Reading on 26 July was opened by H. Linstead and closed by H. Willink (H.C. Debates, Vols. 422 & 426). During the 1945-6 Session, Richard Law was Joint Chairman of the Conservative Housing and Health Committee with special responsibility for health matters. Henry Willink had been Conservative Minister of Health during the wartime Coalition and the 1945 'Caretaker' Governments and was therefore well qualified to speak for the Opposition on this Bill.

The latter part of 1946 witnessed the Second Reading of the Transport Bill. The Opposition case was opened on 16 December by Maxwell Fyfe, Chairman of the Conservative Transport Committee during 1946, and closed on 18 December by Eden. During 1947, W. S. Morrison led a concerted Opposition attack on the Town and Country Planning Bill, opening the debate on Second Reading on 29 January and also the Third Reading on 20 May. The Second Reading on this Bill was followed some few days later by the Second Reading debate on the Electricity Bill, opened on 3 February by Robert Hudson. Two further important measures of nationalization were considered by the Opposition during 1948. On 19 February, Brendan Bracken opened for the Conservatives on the Second Reading of the Gas Bill. This measure apparently met with a much fiercer opposition than that which the Bill on electricity had done, some 127 hours being devoted to the Committee stage of the Bill (Bulmer-Thomas, ii, 170; Hoffman, 246). As upon so many other Bills considered during these years, Bracken, as principal Opposition Spokesman, was also Chairman of the relevant Conservative Back-bench Committee, chairing the Fuel and Power Committee between 1947 and 1950.

The nationalization of iron and steel was the keystone in the Government's programme and was challenged at all stages by the Opposition. As we have seen, Oliver Lyttelton was the Shadow Minister responsible for putting the Conservative case on this issue. He opened on both the Second and Third Readings of the Iron and Steel Bill, the winding up speeches being made by Eden and Peake (H.C. Debates, Vols. 458 & 464). The Bill was fought out line by line at the Committee stage, the Committee meeting on some thirty-six occasions with the bulk of the work being done by Lyttelton himself, Macmillan and Manningham-Buller (Chandos, 335). The prolonged struggle over steel highlighted the wider constitutional issue of the future of the House of Lords. The Government, fearing that the Upper House might reject the Steel Bill, introduced a Bill to amend the 1911 Parliament Act thereby further reducing the delaying power of the House of Lords. At the suggestion of the Opposition, an inter-Party Conference was set up to consider the issue, the Conservative side being represented by four members of the Shadow Cabinet, Eden, Salisbury, Swinton and Maxwell Fyfe. Although the Lords did put forward a substantial number of amendments, they did not reject the Bill outright.

Approach of the 1950 General Election

The Shadow Cabinet co-ordinated and guided the activities of the various parts of the Conservative Party machine between 1945-51 and was undoubtedly the keystone of the whole Opposition structure. We have seen already that its members were the Chairmen of the various Party Committees. Another of its members, R. A. Butler, was Chairman of the very important Research Department which played a vital part in the Conservative recovery. The Research Department absorbed two other important bodies in 1948, namely the Parliamentary Secretariat and the Library, the former having been established to work alongside the Shadow Cabinet preparing briefs on day to day issues arising in Parliament (Hoffman, 72). Two other members of the Shadow Cabinet, Woolton and Maxwell Fyfe were involved in the vitally important overhaul of the Party structure and image. Without the efforts of these two men the work of the Party in Parliament might well have gone by default. The Opposition was, in fact, denied victory at the 1950 Election, but made a substantial recovery over 1945, winning some 298 seats, 17 less than the Labour Party. In the face of increased Opposition pressure, the Government contrived to last some twelve months longer, Parliament finally being dissolved in the Autumn of 1951.

When the Election was held on 25 October, the Conservatives were returned to power with 321 seats against 294 Labour and 6 Liberals. Churchill decided that half of his Cabinet should be people who had never held office before. He was also determined to bring in people who had made reputations outside Parliament and who might consequently give breadth to his administration (Woolton, 363-4). However, when the Prime Minister announced the names of his colleagues, the principal portfolios were distributed between members of the Shadow Cabinet. W. S. Morrison became Speaker of the House of Commons.

Yet another, Lord Swinton, entered the Cabinet in November 1952. As expected, Eden became Foreign Secretary. Previously, he had been Foreign Secretary between 1940-5 and throughout the years of Opposition between 1945-51 had been Chairman of the Conservative Foreign Affairs Committee. Harold Macmillan became Minister of Housing and Local Government and James Stuart went to the Scottish Office. During the 1950-1 Session, Macmillan had been Chairman of the Conservative Housing Committee and Stuart, Chairman of the Scottish Unionist Members' Committee. Of the others, Butler became Chancellor of the Exchequer, Lyttelton went to the Colonial Office, Crookshank to the Ministry of Health and Maxwell Fyfe to the Home Office (where, also, he was made responsible for Welsh affairs). Lord Salisbury became Lord Privy Seal, then went to the Commonwealth Relations Office and, in November 1952, was appointed Lord President of the Council. Between 1940-5, Salisbury, then Viscount Cranborne, had been Secretary of State for the Dominions. Lord Swinton succeeded Salisbury at the Commonwealth Relations Office.

6
The Modern Shadow Cabinet

Over the years since the Shadow Cabinet saw its origins in the ex-Cabinets and quasi-Cabinets of the nineteenth-century Whigs and Tories, the increasing role and importance of a co-ordinated and effective Opposition has been seen to be vital to the system of Parliamentary democracy which we know in Britain. Apart from its role of opposing, it has also been found necessary to put forward viable alternative proposals for government. In other words, the Opposition has had to be responsible as well as critical.

The period from 1951 to 1964 saw the functioning of a distinct two-party system, the Liberals playing only a minor role in national politics with six members in the House of Commons. The Labour Opposition had ample opportunity to study the best and most effective ways of organizing its forces with the result that a distinct Shadow Cabinet and, indeed, Shadow Government system emerged. This is not to say that the Labour Party found its task an easy one. Indeed, for some years after the 1951 Election defeat there was considerable internal conflict amongst the Party leadership. During part of this period, Aneurin Bevan and a number of his supporters constituted what was practically a 'shadow Shadow Cabinet' (Shinwell, 1963, 193). It was, therefore, only comparatively slowly that the Labour Party put its house in order and attained the degree of organization evident by the early 1960s. There have since been a number of incidents and clashes between personalities but these have been dealt with firmly by the Party leaders. Some of the most savage conflicts have involved the attitude of the Labour Party towards defence and military policy, formerly over Germany and the question of re-armament and, more recently, over disarmament and the nuclear arms race. The choosing of Party leaders has also been a source of disunity and embarrassment with both public and private exhibitions of canvassing on behalf of one or another of the candidates, although this is equally true of democratic political parties throughout the world.

Divided we fall

This study has recognized a number of operational and institutional similarities between the Cabinet and the Shadow Cabinet. Indeed, it has been suggested that the Opposition requires almost exactly the same qualities a Government itself requires (Laski, 175-6). In the light of this statement, it is worth asking whether there is any element of collective responsibility in Opposition. Do Shadow Cabinets attempt to follow any such doctrine? By their very nature, Shadow Cabinets consist of teams with recognized leaders who both expect and receive loyalty and support from their colleagues. However, a point can be reached where a person cannot reconcile his views with those of his colleagues in the Shadow Cabinet. In such cases, one of two courses is open, either to accept the fact that a difference exists and leave the matter there or, in extreme cases, to resign. The consequences of 'resignations' from a Shadow Cabinet may not be as serious as those resulting from resignations in a Cabinet, but the principles are the same. The attitude, 'united we stand, divided we fall', is just as relevant to Opposition leaders as it is to the Government. Although they do not have so far to 'fall', being already out of office, the Opposition leaders undoubtedly wish to retain the support of their close colleagues and so be at the head of their 'troops' when, and if, they return to power. The unity of the Shadow Cabinet is increasingly being considered as important as that of the Government by both the press and television, differences of opinion and hints of real or apparent splits being rapidly and ruthlessly examined. This acceptance of collective responsibility has recently been described as 'one of the most important elements in the twentieth-century development of the Shadow Cabinet' (Cross & Alderman, 69). In view of the intensity of some of these conflicts within the ranks of the P.L.P. in Opposition, it is surprising that only two actual 'resignations' occurred in the Shadow Cabinet between 1951 and 1964. Aneurin Bevan resigned in April 1954 over the creation of the South East Asia Treaty Organization (SEATO) and American policy in South-East Asia. The other resignation was that of Anthony Greenwood in October 1960 over Hugh Gaitskell's leadership and 'Clause Four' of the Labour Party Constitution.

Bevan, Greenwood and Crossman

As already indicated, Bevan and his supporters often found themselves in conflict with the official views of the Labour Party. The 'Bevanite' group was very influential on the National Executive Committee, gaining a majority of the seats reserved for the Constituency parties. In March 1952, during a debate on re-armament, the serious split between the leadership and the 'Bevanites' came into the open, with 57 Labour M.P.s going against the advice of the Party leadership and voting against the Government (Shinwell, 1963, 194). The considerable influence of Bevan during this period was illustrated by his election to the Shadow Cabinet for the first time in November 1952. Membership of this body did not prevent Bevan from

60

pressing home his attacks on various aspects of Party policy and, as we have already seen, he resigned in April 1954 following a particularly bitter outburst in the House of Commons over the creation of SEATO (*The Times*, 14 April 1954). There was further trouble in May during the debates on the Atomic Energy Bill, when Bevan and 63 supporters, including three Opposition Whips, went against the Front Bench by supporting an amendment moved by F. Beswick (*The Times*, 4 May 1954). In 1955, the Shadow Cabinet was divided over a call to withdraw the Whip from Bevan. When the issue was put before the P.L.P. as a whole the result was very close with 141 in favour and 112 opposed to any such action (Shinwell, 1963, 194-5).

When Attlee resigned as Leader in December 1955, Bevan was one of the three challengers for the vacancy. Although heavily beaten for first place by Gaitskell, Bevan received 30 more votes than the current Deputy Leader, Herbert Morrison a further indication of the influence his group had in the P.L.P. as a whole. However, he was also defeated for the Deputy Leadership, this time by James Griffiths. Bevan and Gaitskell contrived to bury their differences and in 1957 Gaitskell asked Bevan to become Shadow Foreign Secretary, a responsibility he retained until 1959. Following the Labour Party's third electoral defeat in 1959, Gaitskell set about revising the image and policies of the Party and, in particular, the controversial 'Clause Four' concerning public ownership. Evidently this was done without consulting either the Shadow Cabinet or the N.E.C., and caused a good deal of unrest in the Party as a whole. In March 1960 there was another sizeable revolt in the House of Commons when 43 members abstained on the official Opposition amendment to the Government's Defence White Paper. One of the abstainers was R. Crossman, a Front Bench spokesman on Pensions and National Insurance. Not surprisingly, Crossman was rebuked by his Leader and withdrew from the Front Bench. In his letter to Crossman, published in *The Times*, Gaitskell recognized that Opposition spokesmen might sometimes differ from the views of the majority, but stressed that such differences should not be expressed in public (*The Times*, 15 March 1960). Some seven months later the conflict over defence policy, linked with criticism of Gaitskell's leadership, led to the resignation of Anthony Greenwood from the Shadow Cabinet. Greenwood, who had first been elected to the Shadow Cabinet in November 1951, was replaced by the former Front Bench spokesman, Richard Crossman, who had taken thirteenth place in the poll held in November 1959. In his letter of resignation to Gaitskell, Greenwood stated that he had not decided to resign over the defence issue alone, but because he believed that Gaitskell had divided the Party and that his decision to challenge the Party Conference would lead the Party to disaster (*The Times*, 14 October 1960).

Checks and balances

What is the relationship of the Shadow Cabinet to the remainder of the Labour Party? There has long been argument over the division of power between the parliamentary and extra-parliamentary sections of the Party. This is only natural, the Labour Party having its origins in the labour organizations and socialist societies outside Parliament. There has always been a strong element of extra-parliamentary control and pressure over the actions of the P.L.P. and hence over the Leader and members of the Shadow Cabinet. As the P.L.P. grew in stature and achieved a position of power and importance in British politics, constituting first the official Opposition and later the Government, so it tended to resent what it regarded as interference in the execution of its parliamentary duties by the main body of the Party outside Parliament. R. T. McKenzie considers that the P.L.P. has gradually removed itself from what he calls the 'excessive extra-parliamentary control, as laid down in the Party Constitution and so been able to provide both a strong Government in 1945 and also an effective Shadow Cabinet' (McKenzie, *Political Studies*, Vol. V, 1957). However, the Shadow Cabinet must, and does, work closely with the N.E.C., which is in control of the day to day running of the national Party organization, and also the Trades Unions.

The N.E.C., like the Shadow Cabinet, is elected annually, though by the Party Conference and not the Parliamentary Party. It consists of 25 members, a Treasurer, and the Leader and Deputy Leader of the Party, who are both *ex officio* members of the Committee. Upon examining the composition of the N.E.C. elected for 1963-4, one is immediately struck by the predominance of members of the P.L.P. There were sixteen members of Parliament in addition to the Leader and Deputy Leader of the Party. Two of these, J. Callaghan and R. Gunter were elected members of the Shadow Cabinet, whilst Miss A. Bacon, Miss M. Herbison, Mrs E. White, F. Mulley and R. Crossman were all Front Bench spokesmen during 1963-4. The Trades Unions, with twelve members, constituted the largest individual group, or division, though even here, four were members of the P.L.P. It is also interesting to note the prominent place given on the N.E.C. to women, six serving during the 1963-4, a marked contrast to the membership of the Shadow Cabinet which has only contained one woman in its entire history, Dr E. Summerskill (Baroness Summerskill), between 1951-7 and 1958-9.

The Party Conferences provide an annual opportunity for a gathering of all the various sections of the Labour Party. Members of the Shadow Cabinet and the N.E.C. attend the Conferences in an *ex officio* capacity. Both the N.E.C. and the P.L.P. present reports to the Conference which are open to debate. Very prominent in the Conference deliberations, and indeed in the whole Labour movement, are the Trades Unions with their numerical strength and financial power. The relations between the P.L.P., the N.E.C. and the Trades Unions have, as McKenzie, points out, always been close, 'a review of the record of the N.E.C. showing that it has never attempted to move in any direction in which a majority of affiliated trades unions were not prepared to follow' (McKenzie, 519-20). Further evidence of the close co-operation between the P.L.P. and the N.E.C. is that provided by the compilation of Party Manifestos. During the press conference convened for the launching of the 1964 Manifesto on 11 September, H. Wilson referred to the question of power and decision-making in the Labour Party. He stated that the Manifesto, the combined product of the N.E.C. and the Shadow Cabinet, was the programme for a Labour Government. He made it clear, however, that a Labour Government would be master of its own house, stating that the N.E.C. and the Shadow Cabinet had neither the constitutional power nor the moral authority to decide the order of priorities in the programme of a Labour Government prior to its taking office (*Daily Telegraph*, 12 September 1964). The Labour Party Constitution states that:

the N.E.C. and the Parliamentary Committee of the P.L.P. shall decide which items from the Party programme shall be included in the Manifesto which shall be issued by the N.E.C. prior to every General Election. The joint meeting of the two Committees shall also define the attitude of the Party to the principal issues raised by the Election which are not covered by the Manifesto.

Though both H. Wilson and G. Brown contributed to the Manifesto, the major part of the work was undertaken by P. Shore, head of the Party Research Department, and D. Ennals, head of the Overseas and International Department (*The Sunday Times*, 13 September 1964).

It would appear, therefore, that whilst there are a good

64

many extra-parliamentary bodies and individuals contributing to the formulation of Party policy, the parliamentary leaders retain overall control through their *ex officio* membership of every important Party Committee.

Extensive network of Committees

This overall surveillance is even extended to include the various N.E.C. Sub-Committees, on nearly all of which the Leader and Deputy Leader are included, and the P.L.P. Committees, Subject and Area Groups which are chaired by members of the Shadow Cabinet. During 1963-4, the Leader and Deputy Leader were members of the following N.E.C. Sub-Committees:

	Chairman:
Organization	*R. Gunter*
Youth	*Mrs E. Braddock*
Overseas	*W. Padley*
Home Policy	*G. Brown*
Finance and Economic Policy	*I. Mikardo*
Science and Industry	*R. Crossman*
Publicity	*Miss A. Bacon*
Finance and General Purposes	*D. Davies*

The Finance and Economic Policy and the Science and Industry Sub-Committees were composed of N.E.C. members and *co-opted members*. This meant that, in addition to H. Wilson, G. Brown and J. Callaghan, the Finance and Economic Sub-Committee included D. Houghton, D. Jay, F. Lee and G. Mitchison, or, in other words, seven members of the Shadow Cabinet. The Science and Industry Sub-Committee did not include any further members of the Shadow Cabinet, though R. Prentice, a Front Bench spokesman on Labour, was included. The Local Government Sub-Committee included on the N.E.C. side, Miss A. Bacon, Miss M. Herbison and Mrs E. White, who were all Front Bench spokeswomen and, amongst the co-opted members, M. Stewart, J. McColl and C.

Hughes, the Front Bench team on Housing and Local Government. In addition, there were joint N.E.C./P.L.P. Committees on the Air Transport and Aircraft Industries and on Disarmament, the former including G. Brown, Mrs. E. White, F. Lee and J. Cronin, whilst the Committee on Disarmament included P. Gordon Walker, the Shadow Foreign Secretary, G. Brown, D. Healey, the Shadow Defence Minister, F. Mulley, a Front Bench spokesman on Disarmament and the United Nations, and R. Prentice.

The N.E.C. also set up a number of Study Groups which, once again, were divided between members of the N.E.C. and co-opted members. A group on the *Supply of Teachers* included the Front Bench spokesmen on Education (F. Willey and Mrs E. White), Home Office (Miss A. Bacon), Scottish Affairs (Miss M. Herbison) and Science (R. Crossman), whilst a similar group on *Security and Old Age* included six members of the Shadow Cabinet and six Front Bench spokesmen. There were also Groups on *Commonwealth Immigrants* and on *Crime Prevention and Penal Reform (Labour Party Conference Report, 1964)*.

The Study Group on the *Supply of Teachers* received a considerable amount of publicity during May 1964. Richard Crossman, the Shadow Minister of Science and Chairman of the Group, was reprimanded by the Party hierarchy for presenting the conclusions of the Group to a press conference as *official* Labour Party policy. The suggestion which caused particular unrest was one which proposed half-day schooling for children under six years of age. Mr Crossman stated at the press conference that the N.E.C. had studied the plan and a ten point summary and accepted 'both its analysis and conclusion', the Report evidently being introduced as the 'Labour Party's new plan' (*Daily Herald*, 14 May 1964). Harold Wilson and the Shadow Cabinet, influenced by the militant reception which the idea received from the Labour back-benches, were quick to deny official backing for the Crossman plan. However, *The Times* was somewhat surprised by this denial on the part of the Shadow Cabinet, stating that alongside Crossman on the platform at the press conference had been G. Brown, F. Willey, Mrs E. White and A. Greenwood, the Chairman of the Party. In addition, F. Willey and Mrs E. White, the principal Opposition spokesmen on Education had both been present at the meeting of Labour back-bench M.P.s concerned with education (Mr Willey was Chairman) which called for the rejection of the scheme. It was confirmed later that the Plan had not, in fact, been studied by the N.E.C. as claimed by Crossman, or by the P.L.P. (*The Times*, 14 May 1964). The B.B.C. television programme *Gallery*, on 14 May, included an interview with Mr Crossman in which he stated that what had been studied by the Home Policy Sub-Committee of the N.E.C. (and circulated to the full N.E.C.) was a summary which he had prepared himself for the convenience of the Committee. The Shadow Cabinet met after the back-bench group had completed their discussion on the matter, Crossman not being invited to the meeting or, evidently, consulted by the Leader of the Opposition (*The Sunday Times*, 17 May 1964). There the issue rests, but it is interesting to note the part the Labour back-benchers played in killing the idea and the overall authority exercised by the Shadow Cabinet. It would appear that there was either a serious lack of co-ordination and communication between the Party leaders, or else a rapid application of some principle of '*collective responsibility*' on the part of the Shadow Cabinet with Mr Crossman being 'sacrificed' as the author of an electorally unpopular idea.

A considerable amount of time and energy is now also devoted by small groups and committees within the P.L.P. to considering initial policy drafts which are then submitted to the Shadow Cabinet for amendment and approval before being presented to full meetings of the P.L.P. At these meetings of the P.L.P., members of the

Shadow Cabinet apparently sit together at one end of the room facing the main body of members. During the Session 1962-3, the P.L.P. had sixteen such Subject Groups, each of which was normally chaired by the respective Shadow spokesman for that subject. In addition, there were ten Area Groups and *ad hoc* working Groups or parties which gave detailed attention to each major item of legislation (Richards, 104-5 and 115). During the Session 1963-4, there were fifteen P.L.P. Subject Groups, eight of which were chaired by members of the Shadow Cabinet. Another four were chaired by Front Bench spokesmen.

7
Election and selection

Democratic principles demand that leadership at all
levels be elective, that it be frequently renewed,
collective in character, weak in authority.

Duverger, *Political Parties*

Previous ministerial experience is obviously a great asset
when an Opposition party is called upon to form a
Government. Shadow Cabinets, therefore, usually contain
as many experienced members as possible. Prior to the
1964 General Election, Harold Wilson had a distinct
advantage over Labour's first Prime Minister, MacDonald,
who was very limited in his choice of colleagues for
office. It cannot be said that Wilson was endowed with
a profusion of experienced former Ministers upon whom
to call, but the long years in Opposition had provided
ample time to blood possible aspirants for inclusion in
the Government. In addition, Wilson had served in a
Cabinet before, as had Patrick Gordon Walker. There
were also a number of former Labour Ministers not serving
in the Shadow Cabinet who might have been called upon
for advice and assistance in both Houses of Parliament.
In contrast to both MacDonald and Wilson, Attlee had
no lack of experienced colleagues upon whom to call in
1945. Of the ten members of the Shadow Cabinet, elected
in 1939, included in the 1945 Attlee administration, six
had gained experience of office in the wartime Coalition
Government.

Conservative and Labour Leaders both appoint their
own ministerial colleagues when in office, whilst the Con-

servative Leader also retains this prerogative when in Opposition, his Shadow Cabinet becoming the 'ruling oligarchy of the party' (McKenzie, 21). The administrative arrangements of the Labour Party, on the other hand, are geared to a system of elections for all the major offices. The Labour Shadow Cabinet, known originally as the Parliamentary Executive Committee and changed in 1951 to the Parliamentary Committee to avoid confusion with the National Executive Committee, consists of twelve Labour M.P.s elected by fellow members of the P.L.P. with seats in the House of Commons, plus six *officio* members, the Leader and Deputy Leader, the Chief Whip, the Leader of the Labour Peers, the Peers' Whip and their elected representative. The method of voting for the places in the Shadow Cabinet is that each member votes for as many candidates as there are seats, thereby building up a preference table from one to twelve. This method is supposed to prevent splinter groups from concentrating their votes in favour of particular people. If there is a death or resignation from the Shadow Cabinet, then the person who received the thirteenth highest number of votes moves automatically into the vacated post McKenzie, 413). The elected and *ex officio* members of the Shadow Cabinet, with the exception of the Peers, sit on the Opposition Front Bench where they are joined by the Whips and those persons whom the Leader has asked to serve as Front Bench Spokesmen on specific topics. Since these various non-elected spokesmen are the personal appointees of the Party Leader, he is allowed the relative luxury of individual choice, in one respect, similar to that enjoyed by Conservative Leaders of the Opposition. The Opposition Peers have their own Front Bench, though Party organization in the Upper House is less formal than in the House of Commons.

Lord Morrison deplores increasing formalization

The period since the P.L.P. became the official Opposition in 1922 has witnessed a steady increase in the degree of administrative formalization present in the Shadow Cabinet. This trend has been deplored by, amongst others, the late Lord Morrison of Lambeth, who regarded the development as confusing and unnecessary.

The creation of an elected Parliamentary Committee in 1923 was a practical necessity. As we have seen, there were no ex-Ministers who could have formed this central and co-ordinating Committee. If there had been such a pool of ex-Ministers, it can be argued that the practice of electing members to the Shadow Cabinet might never have developed. However, once the Labour Party had formed a Government, the situation became rather confused since there was now both an elective system and the requisite body of ex-Ministers available for inclusion in a Shadow Cabinet. Lord Morrison refers to difficulties in choosing between ex-Ministers and the elected members of the Shadow Cabinet for debates, difficulties which Attlee attempted to solve just prior to his retirement in 1955. He proposed that the Leader of the Opposition should formally designate members of the Front Bench who should on most occasions be the Party's spokesmen when a particular Department or subject was under discussion in the House of Commons (Morrison, 349). Attlee's scheme tended to increase the confusion since back-benchers were now also eligible to speak from the Opposition Front Bench. The Leader was free to appoint whosoever he liked to 'shadow' a specific subject. It made no difference whether the person concerned was an ex-Minister, an elected member of the Shadow Cabinet or a back-bencher. As Lord Morrison has pointed out, this led to a 'good deal of flitting between the back-benches and the Front Bench'.

P.L.P. Opposition Front Bench 1951-64

The period between 1951 and 1964 can be divided into two parts. Between 1951 and Attlee's retirement from the leadership in July 1955, the bulk of the work on the Opposition Front Bench was carried out by the eighteen members of the Shadow Cabinet, a number of whom were ex-Ministers. As we have seen, there was no specific allocation of responsibilities, though certain persons were recognized as specialists in various subjects. However, from 1955 onwards the Opposition Front Bench grew quite rapidly in size with the implementation of Attlee's system of specialized Front Bench Spokesmen. An examination of the membership provides quite an amount of useful information about the Labour Shadow Cabinets between 1951 and 1964. For example, certain members have long terms of service to their credit, J. Callaghan being elected every year throughout the entire period under consideration, Dr Edith Summerskill, A Robens, P. Noel-Baker, E. Shinwell and Sir F. Soskice also being prominent over a long period of time. In addition, the Leadership has shown a remarkably stable pattern with Clement Attlee serving for twenty years as Leader and four years as Deputy Leader under Lansbury, whilst Hugh Gaitskell held office from 1955 to 1963. Since 1923, there have been seven Deputy Leaders, the longest serving being A. Greenwood from 1935 to 1945 and H. Morrison from 1945 until 1955. Hugh Gaitskell was elected in December 1955, together with the new Deputy Leader, James Griffiths, who replaced Herbert Morrison. Between 1951 and 1955, Griffiths had consistently been at the top of the Parliamentary Committee polls, taking first place between 1951 and 1953 and tying for first place in 1954. At the poll taken in June 1955, Griffiths once again took first place ahead of his future leader. W. Whiteley, who had served as Chief Whip in the House of Commons since 1942, died in 1955, being replaced by H. Bowden. This meant, taken overall, that there were no less than twelve changes in the composition of the Shadow Cabinet from that which had served in 1954. K. Younger and T. Fraser, as runners-up in the poll, were automatically included upon the promotion of Gaitskell and Griffiths to the Leadership and Deputy Leadership. H. Dalton, J. Chuter Ede, W. Glenvil Hall and E. Shinwell, all of whom had served continuously since 1951, were excluded and, in fact, were never again elected to serve on the Parliamentary Committee. A. Bevan, A. Greenwood and R. Stokes were re-elected, having previously served in 1953 and 1951 respectively. Sir Frank Soskice, who had taken third place in the poll in both 1953 and 1954, was not elected, though he returned in 1956 to continue without break until 1964. The two remaining changes were G. Brown and G. Mitchison, neither of whom had previously secured election to the Committee.

Between 1955 and 1959, there were very few changes in the membership of the Shadow Cabinet, Sir F. Soskice replacing R. Stokes in November 1956, A. Bottomley and P. Gordon Walker replacing Dr Summerskill and K. Younger in November 1957, and G. Brown being omitted in November 1958. The year 1959 saw the defeats of the long serving P. Noel-Baker and Dr Summerskill (who had been re-elected in 1958) whilst A. Bottomley lost his Commons seat in the General Election held that year. In addition, A. Bevan replaced T. Griffiths as Deputy Leader and G. Brown regained the place which he had lost in 1958. Seven Labour M.P.s were given Front Bench status for the first time, F. Willey, F. Lee, D. Healey, R. Crossman, A. Wedgwood Benn, C. Mayhew and Mrs B. Castle, the first four being elected to serve on the Parliamentary Committee. The following year, three more new members were elected to serve on the Committee, R. Gunter, D. Houghton and M. Stewart, Houghton having previously been a spokesman on Pensions and National Insurance with R. Crossman, whilst Stewart had been a spokesman on

Housing and Local Government. An element of continuity and stability was introduced in the polls for the Parliamentary Committee held on 16 November 1961, no new persons being elected, though there was a certain amount of movement in the actual placings. H. Wilson moved from ninth to first place in the poll, D. Houghton from tenth to third, J. Callaghan slipping from first to seventh place. The Leader, Deputy Leader and Chief Whip were all challenged during the elections, Gaitskell by Greenwood, Brown by Mrs Castle and Bowden by B. Parkin, none of the challengers getting within 100 votes of their rivals. The continuity was not disturbed in 1962, the same twelve members being re-elected. There was, however, the familiar re-allocation of Opposition *portfolios* which was announced in February 1963. P. Gordon Walker replaced H. Wilson on Foreign Affairs, D. Healey took over from Gordon Walker as Defence Spokesman, whilst A. Bottomley replaced Healey on Colonial Affairs. There were also three new appointments, C. Pannell on Public Building and Works, D. Houghton on Treasury Affairs (acting as a Shadow Chief Secretary) and P. Noel-Baker on Disarmament and the United Nations. A. Bottomley had been returned to Parliament, and hence the Opposition Front Bench, at a by-election for Middlesborough East in 1962. The Parliamentary Committee elections in November 1963 returned the same men to office, though there were seventeen unsuccessful candidates, including well known figures such as R. Crossman, the Front Bench Spokesman on Science, A. Greenwood, the Party Chairman, A. Wedgwood Benn, tipped by many people to gain a place on the Committee following his 'reluctant Peer' struggle, and A. Bottomley. Once again, no women were successful, the nearest contenders being Mrs B. Castle at number twenty-three in the poll, Mrs J. Hart in twenty-fifth place and Miss A. Bacon in twenty-sixth place. One of the most surprising features of the ballot was the number of votes obtained by M. Stewart, who progressed from eighth place

74

in 1962 to head the poll. The complete list of placings and votes received was as follows:

P.L.P. Parliamentary Committee Election 1963

		votes			votes
1st	M. Stewart	(184)	7th	D. Healey	(143)
2nd	J. Callaghan	175	8th	R. Gunter	137
3rd	D. Houghton	164	9th	F. Lee	135
4th	Sir F. Soskice	159	10th	F. Willey	135
5th	P. Gordon Walker	156	11th	D. Jay	130
6th	T. Fraser	146	12th	G. Mitchison	123

Opposition 'double banking'

A feature worthy of note during these years was the existence of some kind of 'double banking' on the Opposition Front Bench. For example, two members of the Shadow Cabinet elected in November 1963 were concerned with the Treasury, J. Callaghan and D. Houghton. Members of the Shadow Cabinet were often assisted by Front Bench spokesmen. P. Gordon Walker (Foreign Affairs) was supported by C. Mayhew, whilst F. Willey (Education) was supported by Mrs E. White. D. Healey (Defence) was aided by Front Bench Spokesmen on Aviation (J. Cronin), Admiralty (G. Willis) and the War Office (R. Paget). Three spokesmen were concerned with the Commonwealth, Colonies and Colonial Relations, A. Bottomley, G. Thomson and A. Creech Jones, though none was a member of the Shadow Cabinet. Most of the other Departments were *shadowed* by two or more Front Bench spokesmen. A similar arrangement had been in operation during earlier years. During 1959-60, the Foreign Office had been *shadowed* by A. Bevan (Deputy Leader) and D. Healey, both members of the Shadow Cabinet, supported by P. Noel-Baker. J. Callaghan (Colonies) had been assisted by A. Creech Jones and G. Thomson (Colonies) and H. Marquand (Colonial Relations). P. Gordon Walker (Home Office) was aided by Miss A. Bacon and E. Fletcher, whilst

H. Wilson (Treasury and Board of Trade) was supported by D. Jay and R. Jenkins. In most cases, the persons asked to *shadow* specific subjects specialize in these fields. However, spokesmen do sometimes open debates and lead Opposition attacks on subjects different to those which they normally cover. For example, in the debate on Estimates for the Ministry of Transport, R. Gunter, the Shadow Minister of Labour opened for the Opposition on 8 July 1964, whilst in the debate on the North East of England on 16 July, F. Willey, the Shadow Minister of Education opened for the Opposition. It should be stated here, however, that Willey was the Member for Sunderland North.

Referring to this question of which people shall speak during a particular debate, Peter G. Richards has stated that, 'choice of those who are called to participate in debates rests entirely upon the discretion of the Speaker, but it is also conditioned by convention'. During the Session 1963-4, members of the Shadow Cabinet and Front Bench restricted themselves almost completely to their respective *Shadow* subjects and only on rare occasions did they depart from this pattern. In some instances, two members of the Shadow Cabinet took part in the same debate, the one opening and the other closing the Opposition case, though in the majority of instances one member of the Shadow Cabinet took part, supported by a Front Bench spokesman on the same subject. The more senior of the two spokesmen generally opened the Opposition case, the closing speech being made by the secondary spokesman. In those cases where no member of the Shadow Cabinet was directly concerned, such as Commonwealth, Colonies and Colonial Relations, then the Front Bench spokesmen were in full control, briefed beforehand, no doubt by the Shadow Cabinet. Arthur Bottomley, for example, led for the Opposition during the debates at Second Reading on five Bills concerning the Commonwealth. F. Peart was undoubtedly the principal spokesman on Agriculture, as was K. Robinson on Health, R. Crossman on Science and W. Ross on Scottish Affairs. Only occasionally were other Labour Members invited to open or close debates, though three former Ministers, E. Shinwell, J. Chuter Ede and A. Woodburn did each close a debate during the Session. F. Bellinger, a former Secretary of State for War, also opened a Supply debate on overseas military expenditure on 6 May 1964. Of the other Labour Members who were invited to speak from the Opposition Front Bench, at least ten became Ministers in the 1964 Government. For example, D. Howell (U.S. Ministry of Education and Science) took part in the debate on Leisure and Sport on 22 June. G. Reynolds (U.S. for Defence (Army)) spoke on service matters upon a number of occasions, whilst J. Diamond, who became Chief Secretary to the Treasury, spoke during the Second Reading of the Finance Bill on 7 May 1964. Throughout the Sessions, therefore, there was in operation a particularly rigid and clearly defined Opposition machine in which members of the Shadow Cabinet and Front Bench were predominant.

Approach of the 1964 General Election

As the date of the 1964 Election drew nearer, so the amount of press, television and radio coverage grew in intensity. It was announced in mid-September that there would be thirteen party political broadcasts before the Election. These were to consist of five each for the Conservative and Labour Parties and three for the Liberal Party. The programmes were all to be screened at 9.30 p.m. There were, in addition, to be seven sound broadcasts each for the major Parties and four for the Liberals. All these programmes were in addition to a comprehensive range of political programmes by the B.B.C. and I.T.V. Newspapers began to devote more and more space to articles about the relative merits of the various Party policies and personalities. A favourite pastime was to predict the shape of a future Labour Government, assum-

77

ing that the Labour Party won the Election. Undoubtedly, the first major salvo of the campaign was fired by the Opposition with the publication on 11 September 1964 of the Labour Election Manifesto, *The New Britain*, a short, concise document of some 8,000 words which appears to have been well received by the Press. The contents of the Manifesto were immediately published in the newspapers and analysed in some depth by the various editors and political commentators. The Labour Party followed up a Press Conference with a television broadcast the same evening. Following the publication of the Labour Party Manifesto and Harold Wilson's briefing of all the Party candidates at Congress House on 13 September, an announcement was made on Tuesday, 15 September by the Prime Minister from 10 Downing Street, that the General Election would be held on Thursday 15 October 1964. The Leader of the Opposition and the Liberal Leader, J. Grimond, had been notified of the Prime Minister's intentions prior to the public announcement.

It became noticeable during the early months leading up to the Election that great emphasis was being placed by the television channels on identifying the leading members of the Government and the Opposition. The news bulletins screened photographs of Government and Opposition spokesmen and leading members of the Opposition were referred to as *Chief Opposition Spokesman*, *Opposition Spokesman* or *Shadow Minister* of, for example, Labour or Housing and Local Government. To take a typical example, during the B.B.C. Channel 1 news bulletin at 6 p.m. on 15 June, photographs were shown of G. Brown, P. Gordon Walker and A. Bottomley. Programmes such as *Panorama* and *Gallery* introduced the general viewing public to leading members of the Government and the Opposition, making extensive use of interviews, cross-examinations and discussion groups. The viewer was made to feel part of the whole proceeding by adroit use of the cameras and was able to listen to, and watch very carefully, the performances of the respective Party spokesman. As the Election and the summer recess drew nearer, however, both *Panorama* and *Gallery* were taken off the screen, not returning until the middle of September.

Television is said to be a hard taskmaster which will readily expose deficiencies in knowledge and debating ability. The Parties devoted much time, therefore, to streamlining the image and public relations aspects of their respective organizations. The speakers for particular programmes were carefully selected and briefed in an attempt not to harm the Party image in the eyes of the viewing public, the electorate. Occasionally, and often due to unforseen circumstances, things might have gone wrong, with the Press pouncing eagerly upon opportunities to emphasize contradictory policy statements or rash promises made by leading members of the same Party. A Front Bench Spokesman, A. Wedgwood Benn, was the broadcasting adviser for the Opposition, assisted by a fellow Front Bencher, C. Mayhew, and a Committee drawn from the Party and including television experts. The Party political broadcasts generally took the form of personal appearances by the Party Leaders. During the early part of 1964 some *documentary* programmes also began to appear. One such programme by the Labour Party took the form of an attack upon two aspects of Conservative policy, Defence and Housing. Denis Healey, the Shadow Defence Minister, and William Ross gave the respective commentaries to accompany the films. At various times during the early months of 1964, H. Wilson, G. Brown, J. Callaghan, P. Gordon Walker, R. Gunter, M. Stewart, C. Mayhew, K. Robinson, Miss M. Herbison and R. Crossman all appeared on television.

There was, quite naturally, a temporary lull in the proceedings during the summer recess and the general holiday period. However by early September the whole process got under way once more. A Labour Party broadcast was held on 11 September, following the publication of the *The New Britain*, including five leading spokesmen, H. Wilson, J. Callaghan, R. Crossman and M. Stewart from the Shadow Cabinet and also Lord Gardiner, the person generally expected to become Labour Lord Chancellor. The programme took the form of a review of the Manifesto, in which the speakers referred to the various major proposals. It was notable that two of the most important fields, Defence and Foreign Affairs were not included. Once the Election had been fixed for 15 October, it was announced that the B.B.C. would, from 16 September, provide a special service of news and comments on the Election campaign. In addition to the return of *Panorama* and *Gallery*, there were to be extended news bulletins and two new programmes, *Election Forum* and *Question Time*. The former was a programme in which H. Wilson, J. Grimond and Sir Alec Douglas-Home answered viewers' questions, whilst the latter consisted of candidates chosen by the Parties being questioned by a panel of journalists. The radio was similarly to cover the campaign comprehensively with news bulletins, *Radio Newsreel* and *Any Questions*, whilst the I.T.V. networks planned to introduce nightly programmes called *Election '64* which commenced on 28 September.

'Shadows' into realities

Members of Shadow Cabinets naturally hope, in due course, either to return to power or else to achieve power. This is one of the basic tenets of the whole Shadow Cabinet system. Whilst the Labour Party did approach the 1964 Election with the unenviable record of having lost three consecutive General Elections, the main framework for a possible Labour Cabinet was readily available in the Shadow Cabinet and amongst the Front Bench spokesmen and women. In other words, the *shadows* were liable to become *realities*, with the Shadow Ministers crossing the floor of the House of Commons to become the new Cabinet Ministers and members of the Government. It seemed likely that Harold Wilson would rely upon this body of people, but he was also fully justified in making any changes which he felt to be necessary and, indeed, to introduce some new faces into the ranks of a Labour Government.

The retention of the Yorkshire constituency of Penistone, announced during the afternoon of Friday, 16 October 1964, gave the Labour Party the 316 seats necessary to assure them of a majority of seats in the House of Commons. The Election had been even closer than in 1951 when the Conservatives had returned to office with an overall majority of 17 seats. The final figures in October 1964 were Labour 317, Conservatives 303, Liberal 9 and Mr Speaker, giving the Labour Party an overall majority of 4 seats. There was no concession of victory by the Conservatives until it was obvious that they could not obtain the necessary majority of seats. By 3 p.m., however, the Prime Minister, Sir Alec Douglas-Home, must have known that his Government was defeated, and at 3.30 p.m. he arrived at Buckingham Palace to tender his resignation to Her Majesty the Queen. Shortly afterwards, Mr Wilson was summoned to the Palace and invited to form an administration. Thirteen consecutive years on the Opposition Benches had finally ended, with victory at the polls and the formation of only the fourth Labour Government in the twentieth century. Once victory was assured for the Labour Party, speculation as to the composition of the Government became widespread once again. Apart from one or two interesting exceptions, however, the Shadow Cabinet did emerge as the Cabinet. The Prime Minister included every member of his old Shadow Cabinet with the exception of F. Willey (Education), who was made Minister of the new Department of Land and Natural Resources.

With the retirement from the Shadow Cabinet of G.

Mitchison and his subsequent elevation to the House of Lords, his place on the Parliamentary Committee would have been taken by R. Crossman, who had been placed 13th in the poll for election to the Committee for the Session 1963-4. Richard Crossman had been Shadow Minister of Science, but in the Cabinet he changed duties with Michael Stewart, becoming Minister of Housing and Local Government. Herbert Bowden, the Opposition Chief Whip, became Lord President of the Council and Leader of the House, being replaced as Chief Whip by Edward Short. The two other principal changes involved Fred Lee, who moved from Aviation to the Ministry of Power and T. Fraser, who moved from Fuel and Power to the Ministry of Transport. The remaining nine members of the Cabinet of 23, with the exception of Frank Cousins who was brought in from the Trade Unions, had previous parliamentary experience.

Certain other Ministers held Opposition Front Bench posts during the 1963-4 Session, so that in a number of cases, the Shadow Cabinet system was also applied to the Front Bench spokesmen, the new Ministers taking responsibility for the Departments which they had formerly shadowed. In this category we find K. Robinson (Health), C. Pannell (Public Building and Works), Miss A. Bacon (Home Office), G. Darling (Board of Trade), and J. McColl (Housing and Local Government). Quite a number of other Opposition spokesmen were, however, given different posts to those which they had formerly shadowed, such as Miss M. Herbison, Mrs E. White, C. Hughes and F. Mulley.

Some of the remaining Ministers, such as R. Jenkins (Aviation), A. Wedgwood Benn (Postmaster General), E. Fletcher (Minister Without Portfolio), and H. Finch (Parliamentary U.S. Welsh Office) had, in previous years, held Front Bench appointments on various subjects.

Reference has already been made to the reversal of duties in the Cabinet, as compared with Opposition between Stewart and Crossman. It was widely expected that the former would be made Minister of Housing and Local Government, rather than Minister of Education and Science. Michael Stewart had, in fact, shadowed Education during the 1958-9 Session. Similarly, Fred Lee, the Minister of Power, had shadowed his subject during 1959-60. An article in *The Times* on Monday 19 October, discussed the membership of the Wilson Cabinet and the reasons for the composition which had emerged, suggesting that there were a number of factors which had to be taken into account apart from the operation of the Shadow Cabinet system. The main point to emerge was that the composition was both provisional and experimental owing to the dearth of candidates with previous ministerial experience. By creating a large Cabinet of twenty-three persons, the Prime Minister was enabled to 'include almost everybody with a claim, whether it be thought historical, personal, tactical or representative'. The article concluded by making the point that Mr Wilson had 'neatly solved the problem of balancing party forces by basing his Cabinet choices on the movement's elected bodies, the sessionally elected Parliamentary Committee, or Shadow Cabinet, and the National Executive Committee elected by the Annual Conference'. It is true that the Prime Minister balanced the various sectors of the Party inside his Cabinet and did not attempt to remove those colleagues who had been elected to serve on the Shadow Cabinet during the previous Session. It is more doubtful whether the appointments could be called either provisional or experimental. The Cabinet that Mr Wilson established fully justified the existence of a Shadow Cabinet system in British politics and, indeed, it is possible to say that this body, created out of custom, has practically reached the stage of being considered as one of the conventions of Britain's *unwritten* Constitution.

8
Conservatives in Opposition

Following its narrow defeat in the 1964 General Election, the Conservative Party quickly reorganized and attempted to prepare itself for the comparatively unaccustomed role of 'Her Majesty's Opposition'. Speculation and rumour as to the future of the defeated Leader, Sir Alec Douglas-Home, were widespread, as were the probable tactics to be followed by the Conservative Opposition in Parliament. The situation was in many ways similar to that following the electoral defeat in 1945, though the recovery was achieved rather more quickly. Sir Alec Douglas-Home called a meeting of his Shadow Cabinet on Monday, 19 October, some three days after tendering his resignation as Prime Minister to Her Majesty the Queen. Evidently, the meeting consisted of twenty-two former Ministers and took place at the Conservative Research Centre, lasting some forty-five minutes (*The Guardian*, 20 October 1964).

The position of Sir Alec Douglas-Home as Leader was felt in many quarters to be insecure. This was a natural reaction when the Party, like an army, had lost an important battle. Nevertheless, Sir Alec had stated clearly that he would lead the Opposition (*The Times*, 17 October 1964). There had been a certain degree of criticism attached to the choice of Lord Home, first as Foreign Secretary and later as Prime Minister, long-established conventions being broken on both occasions. In fact, he proved stronger and more able than his opponents had anticipated, bringing his Party to the brink of victory from the badly shaken and dispirited state in which it had found itself following the Profumo and national security scandals of the previous summer. This was a remarkable achievement and there was no reason why Sir Alec Douglas-Home should not prove a successful Leader of a powerful and talented Conservative Opposition. Commenting upon the possible composition of Sir Alec Douglas-Home's Shadow Cabinet, the *Daily Telegraph* stated that 'there was no question of an election or selection committee for *shadow* jobs'. It was up to the Party Leader to choose and put forward invitations to persons who specialized in particular subjects. It was felt that the Conservatives would, most probably, utilize the services of former Ministers on the Opposition Front Bench. In those instances where former Ministers had been defeated, then the duties would be undertaken by the respective former Junior Ministers. What did the Leader of the Opposition consider to be the duties of his Shadow administration? In his reply to the Queen's Speech on 3 November, Sir Alec stated that the Opposition would 'judge each proposal on its merits'. He continued, 'the function of the Opposition will be to keep Ministers up to the mark and see that the programmes which we set are fulfilled'. On 5 November, Sir Alec made further references to his plans for the future of the Opposition, stating that his 'recipe for an effective Opposition was teamwork with an infusion of young talent and experience on the Front Bench' (*The Times*, 5 November 1964).

Sir Alec Douglas-Home's Shadow Cabinet

The list of Sir Alec Douglas-Home's Shadow appointments was issued on Wednesday 28 October, being fully reported by the daily press the following morning. However, some of the more predictable appointments had already been discussed, some three days prior to the publication of the official list, by J. Margach in *The Sunday Times* on 25 October. Margach referred to R. Maudling's position as Deputy Leader, E. Heath's role as successor to R. A. Butler on policy, and the return of I. Macleod and E. Powell. It was felt that the influence of R. Maudling would be critical in building up a new team, 'not to fight the last election over again, but to establish new foundations for the next' (*The Sunday Times*, 25 October 1964).

Sir Alec Douglas-Home's Shadow Cabinet *did* consist of experienced former Ministers, though in a number of cases they were asked to shadow posts different to those which they had held whilst in office, notably Sir E. Boyle (Education to Home Affairs), E. Marples (Transport to Technology), S. Lloyd (Lord Privy Seal to Opposition Co-ordinator in the H/C), Sir K. Joseph (Housing, Local Government and Wales to Social Services and Wales) and J. Boyd-Carpenter (Chief Secretary to the Treasury and Paymaster General to Housing and Land). Three former Cabinet Ministers, H. Brooke, F. Erroll and W. Deedes were omitted from the Shadow Cabinet, whilst I. Macleod and E. Powell, both of whom had declined to serve in Sir Alec Douglas-Home's Government returned to the fold to shadow, respectively, Steel and Transport. In addition, there was one newcomer to the ranks of the Front Bench Spokesmen, A. Maude, who was made responsible for Aviation. One or two other interesting points emerged from this list of Conservative Shadow spokesmen. Oppositions need to keep abreast of new developments by the Government of the day. If the Government creates new Departments, then the Opposition feels bound to appoint a Front Bench Spokesman to shadow the new Ministry. Two of Mr Wilson's new Departments were Land and Natural Resources and Overseas Development. The Conservative Opposition appointed Front Bench Spokesmen to shadow both these new Departments, F. Corfield and

R. Carr. Mr Selwyn Lloyd's appointment as 'Co-ordinator of the Opposition in the House of Commons appeared to be rather an unusual responsibility, approximating somewhat to the role of Leader of the House, but in Opposition. There was a certain amount of overlapping with the duties of R. Maudling, whom Sir Alec Douglas-Home had put in charge of parliamentary strategy at Westminster.

Re-allocation of responsibilities

There is no stipulated size for Conservative Shadow Cabinets, the number varying as occasion demands. Members are not required to attend, but normally do so, barring important engagements or duties elsewhere. As in the Cabinet, other persons can be invited to attend for discussion on particular subjects. No formal vote is taken on any decision, the Chairman, normally the Leader, summing up the consensus of opinion in the meeting and acting accordingly. The Conservative Party have never employed the elective principle for the distribution of places in their Shadow Cabinet or Leader's Committee, and it is unlikely that the recent decision to elect by a ballot system, rather than evolve, future Leaders of the Party will in any way alter this arrangement. It is almost certain that, once he has been elected, the Leader of the Conservative Party in Opposition will continue to exercise complete personal discretion in his choice of Shadow Cabinet colleagues. According to the Conservative Opposition Chief Whip, William Whitelaw, although the decision as to who shall speak in a particular debate is a matter for the Leader, the Shadow Cabinet would probably express views about this, and it is customary anyway for the appropriate Front Bench Spokesman to open and wind-up debates on subjects for which they are responsible.

No sooner had the Conservative Opposition formations been settled than a reorganization was necessitated by the withdrawal from active politics of R. A. Butler and the promotion to Party Chairman of Edward du Cann in succession to Lord Blakenham. On 16 February 1965, a revised list of Opposition appointments was announced. There were a number of major changes, R. Maudling taking over Foreign Affairs from R. A. Butler, and E. Heath taking up the reins of Treasury affairs and co-ordination of the so called 'Home field'. The other changes were Sir Edward Boyle (Home Office to Education and Science), P. Thorneycroft (Defence to Home Office), C. Soames (Agriculture to Defence) and Sir M. Redmayne (Post Office to Agriculture). Anthony Barber, the ex-Minister of Health who lost his seat in the General Election, being returned in a subsequent by-election at Altrincham and Sale on 5 February, took over from E. du Cann on Trade matters. Quintin Hogg retained his place in the Shadow Cabinet in order to carry out what was described as *Special Duties*. Sir P. Rawlinson took over Broadcasting, Communications and the Post Office from Sir M. Redmayne but did not become a member of the Shadow Cabinet. His old responsibilities were taken over by W. Roots. Reporting the changes on 17 February, *The Times* commented that they served two main purposes, notably to widen the experience of some of the senior members of the Front Bench, but also to protect certain spokesmen from what was called *Hansardization*, or being reminded too often of what they had said whilst they had been in office. This latter point is most interesting. Obviously, ex-Ministers are the best equipped persons to shadow their old Departments, but the possibility of attacks such as those referred to a little earlier must inevitably exist, though surely with equal severity in the opposite direction. Promises and pledges made whilst in Opposition are often found to be embarrassingly difficult to fulfil in office. This chapter has, so far, been primarily concerned with the responsibilities of the senior Opposition Front Bench spokesmen. However, it should not be overlooked that there was also a

88

considerable network of Junior Opposition spokesmen. On 24 February 1965, Sir Alec Douglas-Home appointed three younger spokesmen who were to be 'second string' Front Benchers, in other words 'double-banking' more senior colleagues. They were P. Emery and P. Walker (Treasury, Economic Affairs and Trade) and J. Biffen (Technology). Mr Biffen's post was formerly the responsibility of D. Price, who was moved to Aviation. In addition, R. Bell took over Labour matters from N. Ridley who retained his responsibility for Power, the two duties having previously been combined. Mr G. Page took over Housing and Land from W. Roots, promoted earlier to succeed Sir P. Rawlinson as one of the Opposition Law spokesmen. Evidently Transport and Aviation were also split, with D. Price taking Aviation (as already mentioned), leaving Transport to T. Galbraith. Mr D. Gibson-Watt was made responsible for Broadcasting and Communications in addition to his Welsh responsibilities. When on 25 February a complete list of Conservative Opposition was issued it had every appearance of being a 'Shadow Government', containing no less than sixty-seven names.

The majority of Senior Opposition Front Bench Spokesmen had at least one junior spokesman to assist them, the only Departments shadowed by a single spokesman being Health (R. Wood), Pensions (Mrs Thatcher), Public Building and Works (J. Ramsden), Land and Natural Resources (F. Corfield) and Overseas Development (R. Carr). Quintin Hogg and Iain Macleod (Special Duties and Steel), often described as two of the Opposition's best 'sharpshooters', were also without assistants. As in the Labour Party, very few places were found on the Opposition Front Bench for women, the Conservatives entrusting only two, Mrs Thatcher and Lady Tweedsmuir, with Opposition responsibilities, Mrs Thatcher on Pensions and Lady Tweedsmuir joining R. Maudling and P. Thomas on Foreign Affairs. Six of the Opposition spokesmen had gained experience of the subjects they were asked to shadow through being associated with Party back-bench Committees on the same subjects. N. Ridley and D. Gibson-Watt had both been Vice Chairman of the Conservative Parliamentary Power and Broadcasting and Communications Committees. W. Clark had been Joint Secretary to the Finance Committee, whilst J. Hall had gained experience on the Trade and Industry Committee. Lord Balniel had been Chairman of the Health and Social Security Committee and Sir J. Eden had been Chairman of the Air Sub-Committee of the Defence Committee. Of the other spokesmen, C. Chataway (Education and Science) had been Joint U.S. for Education and Science during 1964, J. Scott-Hopkins (Agriculture), Fisheries and Food between 1962-4, T. Galbraith (Transport), Joint P.S. at the Ministry of Transport between 1963-4. G. Campbell and J. Stodart (Scottish Affairs) had both been Under Secretaries at the Scottish Office during 1964. P. Thomas (Foreign Affairs) had been Minister of State for Foreign Affairs between 1963-4, whilst N. Fisher (Commonwealth) had been Joint U.S. for Commonwealth Relations and Colonies during 1964. Finally, J. Hay (Navy) had been U.S. of Defence (Navy) during 1964 and N. Wylie (Scottish Law), Solicitor General for Scotland during part of 1964.

As is customary, the Opposition had, during the autumn and early winter, allowed the new Labour Government a short period to settle into office before it commenced to criticize the Government in Parliament. However, when the attack did commence it was felt in many quarters to be lacking in the necessary aggression. The time-worn arguments about how Opposition *should* be conducted were soon in full circulation once again with the political commentators offering advice to Sir Alec Douglas-Home and his Shadow Cabinet colleagues in lengthy and often repetitive columns. Conservative back-benchers also seemed divided over the most suitable course to be adopted, some being restive and 'clearly wanting to fight with the gloves off and to begin without any tactical delay' (*The Times*,

28 October 1964). If, as seems fairly certain, the Opposition had taken things rather too easily before Christmas, the situation soon changed in the months that followed. It was reported in *The Guardian* on 15 March that the Conservatives were to move fully on to the offensive. They apparently aimed to 'break the Government, if necessary by making Parliament impotent (within the rules of procedure) and calculated that a majority of electors would reward them for their work'. There were 60 parliamentary divisions during the first 55 days of the Session, together with a daily average of 180 Parliamentary Questions, but these, at least, did not really appear to worry the Government to any extent. Indeed, a number of older Labour M.P.'s. like E. Shinwell were not at all impressed by the Conservative performance, feeling they had misused chance after chance to embarrass the Government (*The Sunday Times*, 21 February 1965). Undoubtedly, the focal point of the Conservative attack was upon the very long and complicated Finance Bill. However, apart from one tactical defeat in Committee, the Government Whips kept a very close watch on the proceedings. The main Opposition speakers on the Finance Bill were E. Heath, P. Walker and W. Clark.

Edward Heath becomes Leader

Whilst the Labour Government pressed forward with its very considerable programme of legislation, rumours persisted in the ranks of the Opposition throughout the early part of 1965 that Sir Alec Douglas-Home's tenure as Leader of the Opposition would soon be terminated, despite the fact that he appeared intent upon continuing in office and was being publicly and solidly supported by considerable sections of the Conservative Party. Sir Alec Douglas-Home settled the rumours once and for all with an announcement to the massed ranks of the 1922 Committee on Thursday 22 July 1965, that he had resigned as Leader, the

decision apparently stunning many of his back-bench supporters (*The Times*, 23 July 1965). The machinery, as yet
untried, for electing his successor was put into motion
almost immediately. Two contenders in the Shadow
Cabinet clearly stood out over all others, R. Maudling
and E. Heath, though E. Powell finally made the contest
a three-cornered one. The result of the first ballot, on 27
July, gave E. Heath 150 votes, R. Maudling 133 votes and
E. Powell 15 votes. The rules of election required E. Heath,
on the first ballot, to establish a 15 per cent of the total
votes cast lead over R. Maudling. This he failed to do by
28 votes. Technically, further candidates were now free to
seek nomination prior to a second ballot. However, no
second ballot was necessary, both R. Maudling and E.
Powell withdrawing from the contest. The emergence
of a new, elected, Leader meant that there would be still
further re-organization and re-construction within the
Shadow Cabinet. When the revised lists were issued on
4 August 1965, there were no new names but a considerable
interchange of Opposition responsibilities. C. Soames
(Foreign Affairs) also looked after European affairs, whilst
Sir A. Douglas-Home took on the mantle of senior adviser
on the whole range of what was designated 'External
Affairs', which included the Foreign Office, the Commonwealth Relations Office and the Colonial Office. Steel was
no longer a separate responsibility as it was under Sir
Alec Douglas-Home. It was now merged with Trade under
the surveillance of A. Barber. D. Sandys joined Q. Hogg as a
Shadow Minister without a specific 'portfolio'. It is also
noticeable that Conservative Leaders of the Opposition
allocate a separate spokesman for Scottish Affairs, whereas
Welsh Affairs tend to be combined with another subject.
E. Heath appears to have introduced two new concepts
into his Shadow Cabinet, namely the recognition of a
Deputy Leader and the division of the Shadow Cabinet
into three groups covering Overseas Affairs, Economic
Affairs and Social Services (*The Times*, 5 August 1965).

92

On the other hand, it can be argued that these were simply the natural development of ideas originated by Sir Alec Douglas-Home rather than new concepts. To all intents and purposes, R. Maudling had been Deputy Leader to Sir Alec during the latter part of 1964, whilst the list of Opposition responsibilities issued by the Conservative Party on 25 February, had similarly been divided into different sections or groupings of responsibilities. The changes introduced by Edward Heath might well be described as tactical rather than necessary. The emergence of a new Leader called for some public display of power, some tangible evidence that a new man was at the helm.

Heath's 'Shadow Government'

As Parliament broke up for the summer recess, two questions posed themselves. Would E. Heath prove a worthy successor to Sir Alec Douglas-Home and would he prove a match for the Prime Minister? Opinion was widely divided. Mr Heath's initial list of Shadow Cabinet colleagues was soon further enlarged by the announcement on 6 October, of the list of Front Bench Spokesmen. It contained no less than 72 names, making it by far the largest and most comprehensive 'Shadow Administration' in the history of British Parliamentary Opposition. Members of the Shadow Cabinet were assisted by Senior and Junior Spokesmen, thereby providing small specialist groups, or units, on each of the major subjects. For example, C. Soames (Foreign Affairs) was assisted by Lord Balniel and Lady Tweedsmuir, whilst Sir K. Joseph (Labour and Social Services) was joined by R. Wood, G. Howe, C. Longbottom, A. Tiley and W. van Straubenzee The largest groups were overseas (9), Treasury, Economic Affairs and Trade (6), Labour and Social Services (6), De-fence (5) and Housing and Land (4). These were twelve completely new spokesmen and two new Whips, D. Mitchell and G. Younger. Also announced on 6 October was the publication of a new Conservative policy statement, *Putting Britain Right Ahead*. The document, compiled by Mr Heath, was apparently based upon the reports of the various Party Study Groups at the end of their first six months in existence. The Shadow Cabinet had examined the document and had given its approval to the published version (*The Times*, 7 October 1965). Its contents provided the theme for Opposition speeches throughout the country and it was also widely debated at the Annual Party Conference which opened in Brighton on 13 October 1965. During these months E. Heath steadily established himself as Leader of the Party and there were no serious threats to his leadership. However, early in the new year A. Maude, the Front Bench spokesman on the Colonies, published an article in the *Spectator* accusing both the Leader and the Party, as a whole, of lack of initiative. The issue was taken up by the Party and it soon became clear that Mr Maude would not long continue as an Opposition spokesman. The Leader of the Opposition summoned his colleague to a meeting and, following what both later described as a 'friendly discussion', A. Maude announced his return to the back-benches. The Government welcomed this temporary diversion as an opportunity both to gibe at the Opposition's lack of cohesion and also to ease the pressure on their own back-benches. The Government's very slender overall majority in the House of Commons was constantly threatened by the Conservatives. There was also the ever-present danger of sickness amongst some of the older Labour Members of Parliament. It was a most difficult and testing time both for Ministers and Whips intent upon maintaining a satisfactory rate of progress with a very full legislative programme. The Prime Minister was clearly unhappy with such a state of affairs and requested a dissolution of Parliament. A General Election was fixed for 31 March 1966.

The Conservatives and the 1966 General Election

The Labour Party based its election campaign around the need for a clear working majority to enable them to get on with the job of governing. The appeal was a simple one and it proved effective. On the other hand, the Conservative appeal suffered on two counts. When they attacked the Government's record they were accused of being unfair and of not giving it a chance to succeed. When they put forward alternative proposals of their own, they were unable to explain why they had failed to put these proposals into force during their thirteen years in office. The result was a clear-cut victory for the Labour Party which won 363 seats, an increase of 46 over the 1964 Election. The Opposition Front Bench was quite badly mauled, twelve of the team announced by E. Heath in October 1965 losing their seats in Parliament. Three, C. Soames, P. Thorneycroft and Sir M. Redmayne had been members of the Shadow Cabinet, the remaining Front Benchers being J. Amery, W. Clark, P. Emery, J. Scott-Hopkins, P. Thomas, C. Chataway, Lady Tweedsmuir, G. Howe and P. McNair Wilson. The most significant point to emerge from the defeat of the Conservatives was that E. Heath made no attempt to reconstruct his 'Shadow Administration' on the same scale as before. It was announced on 20 April that the new Shadow team included 27 names, excluding the Party Whip. The Shadow Cabinet itself was reduced in size from 21 to 16 and the number of Front Bench spokesmen from 42 to 10. Promoted to the Shadow Cabinet were G. Rippon, Miss M. Pike and P. Walker. Lord Harlech also joined the Shadow Cabinet, replacing Lord Dilhorne as Deputy Leader of the Opposition in the House of Lords. E. Powell retained his place in the Shadow Cabinet with responsibility for Defence matters, whilst S. Lloyd, D. Sandys, J. Boyd-Carpenter and E. Marples returned to the backbenches. The Shadow Defence Minister had provided some moments of tension during the Election campaign with rather outspoken speeches on Vietnam and the question of the Rhodesian oil embargo. The latter speech led to his being cautioned by Mr Heath as to his future conduct if he wished to remain a senior member of the Opposition Front Bench (*The Guardian*), 14 April 1966). The remaining ten Front Bench spokesmen were R. Carr (Aviation), R. Wood (Commonwealth, Colonies and Overseas Development), Sir J. Hobson (Law), P. Bryan (Broadcasting, Communication and Post Office), R. Chichester-Clark (Public Building and Works, Art and Northern Ireland), Lord Balniel (Foreign Affairs), Mrs M. Thatcher (Treasury and Economic Affairs), D. Price (Technology), F. Corfield (Trade and Power) and D. Gibson-Watt (Wales).

Commenting upon the size and membership of the reconstructed Opposition Front Bench, *The Times* pointed out that Mr Heath had taken advantage of the new political situation in which the Conservatives found themselves by selecting a team young enough to take office in the 1970's. The average age of the members of the new Shadow Cabinet was just over forty-eight years.

Bibliography

Books

ALDERMAN, R. and CROSS J. (1967), *The Tactics of Resignation*, Routledge & Kegan Paul

AMERY, L. S. (1953-5), *My Political Life*, 3 vols. Hutchinson

ATTLEE, C. R. (1954), *As it Happened*, Heinemann

BASSETT, R. (1958), *Nineteen Thirty-One: Political Crisis*, Macmillan

BEER, S. (1965), *Modern British Politics*, Faber

BIRKENHEAD, The Earl of (1959), *F.E.*, Eyre & Spottiswoode

BLAKE, R. (1955), *The Unknown Prime Minister*, Eyre & Spottiswoode

BLAKE, R. (1966), *Disraeli*, Eyre & Spottiswoode

BROAD, L. (1955), *Anthony Eden*, Hutchinson

BROMHEAD, P. (1956), *Private Members Bills in the British Parliament*, Routledge & Kegan Paul.

BULMER-THOMAS, I. (1965), *The Growth of the British Party System*, 2 vols. Baker

BUTLER, D. and FREEMAN, J. (1963), *British Political Facts 1900-1960*, Macmillan

BUTLER, D. and FREEMAN, J. (1968), *British Political Facts 1900-1967*, Macmillan

CHAMBERLAIN, SIR A. (1936), *Politics from Inside*, Cassell

CHANDOS, LORD. (1962), *Memoirs*, Bodley Head.

COOKE, C. (1957), *The Life of Richard Stafford Cripps*, Hodder & Stoughton

DERRY, J. (1963), *The Regency Crisis and the Whigs 1788-89*, Cambridge U.P.

DOWSE, R. (1966), *Left in the Centre: the I.L.P. 1893-1940*, Longmans

DUGDALE, B. (1936), *Arthur James Balfour*, 2 vols., Hutchinson

FOORD, A. (1964), *His Majesty's Opposition 1714-1830*, O.U.P.

GARDINER, A. (1923), *The Life of Sir William Harcourt*, 2 vols., Constable

GATHORNE HARDY, A. (1910), *Gathorne Hardy, A Memoir*, Longmans

HARDINGE, SIR A. (1925), *The Fourth Earl of Carnarvon*, O.U.P.

HOFFMAN, J. (1964), *The Conservative Party in Opposition 1945-51*, MacGibbon & Kee

JENKINS, R. (1964), *Asquith*, Collins

KEITH, A. BERRIEDALE (1952), *The British Cabinet System*, Stevens

KILMUIR, LORD. (1962), *Political Adventure*, Weidenfeld & Nicolson

LANG, A. (1891), *Life of Sir Stafford Northcote*, Blackwood

LASKI, H. (1938), *Parliamentary Government in England*, Allen & Unwin

LOWELL, A. (1912), *Government of England*, Macmillan

MCHENRY, D. (1938), *The Labour Party in Transition, 1931-38*, Routledge

MCKENZIE, R. (1958), *British Political Parties*, Heinemann

MACKINTOSH, J. (1962), *The British Cabinet*, Stevens

MAGNUS, SIR P. (1963), *Gladstone*, Murray

MALMESBURY, LORD. (1885), *Memoirs of an Ex-Minister*, Longmans

MIDDLEMAS, R. (1965), *The Clydesiders*, Hutchinson

MITCHELL, A. (1967), *The Whigs in Opposition 1815-30*, O.U.P.

MONYPENNY and BUCKLE, (1929), *Life of Disraeli*, 2 vols., Murray

MORLEY, J. (1903), *Life of Gladstone*, Macmillan

MORRISON OF LAMBETH, LORD. (1959), *Government and Parliament: A Survey from Inside*, O.U.P.

MOWAT, C. (1966), *Britain Between the Wars 1918-40*, Methuen

OXFORD and ASQUITH, The Earl of (1928), *Memories and Reflections*, 2 vols., Cassell

PARKER, C. (1907), *Life of Sir James Graham*, 2 vols., Murray

RICHARDS, P. (1964), *Honourable Members*, Faber

SHINWELL, E. (1963), *The Labour Story*, MacDonald

SPENDER and ASQUITH, (1932), *Life of Oxford and Asquith*, Hutchinson

TAYLOR, H. (1933), *Jix, Viscount Brentford*, Paul

WINTERTON, LORD. (1953), *Orders of the Day*, Cassell

WOOLTON, LORD. (1959), *Memoirs*, Cassell

Articles

ALDERMAN, R. K., 'Parliamentary Party Discipline in Opposition: the P.L.P. 1951-64.' *Parliamentary Affairs*, Vol. XXI, No. 2, 1968

ASPINALL, A., 'English Party Organization in the early Nineteenth Century', *English Historical Review*, July, 1926

ASPINALL. A., (A review of A. S. Foord's book on Opposition), *Parliamentary Affairs*, Vol. XVIII, No. 2, 1965

BEALES, D., A critical review of 'Party Politics' by Sir I. Jennings in *Historical Review*, Vol. 5, No. 2, 1962

BRITTAN, S., 'Some Thoughts on the Conservative Opposition', *Political Quarterly*, Vol. 39, No. 2, 1968

CHESTER, D. N., 'Double Banking and Deputy Ministers', *New Society*, No. 89, June 1964

DOWSE, R. E., 'The P.L.P. in Opposition', *Parliamentary Affairs*, Vol. XIII, 1959-60

FEUCHTWANGER, E., 'The Conservative Party after the 1867 Reform Act', *Victorian Studies*, June 1959

FRASER, P., 'Unionists and Reform: the Crisis of 1906', *Historical Journal*, Vol. 5, No. 2, 1962

HANHAM, H. J., 'Opposition Techniques in Britain', *Government and Opposition*, Vol. 2, No. 1, 1966-67

HORNBY, R., 'Parties in Parliament 1959-63: The Labour Party', *Political Quarterly*, Vol. 34, No. 3, 1963

JENKINS, P., 'Labour's Election Machine', *New Society*, May 1964

MCKENZIE, R. T., 'Policy Decisions in Opposition: a Rejoinder', *Political Studies*, Vol. 5, No. 2, 1957

POWELL, J. ENOCH, 'Labour in Opposition 1951-59', *Political Quarterly*, Vol. 30, 1959

PUNNETT, R., 'The Labour Shadow Cabinet 1955-64', *Parliamentary Affairs*, Vol. XVIII, 1964-65

ROSE, S., 'Policy Decisions in Opposition', *Political Studies*, Vol. 4, 1956

Suggestions for Further Reading

The following works have also been consulted during the course of research for the present volume and may be regarded as useful and relevant additional reading:

AVON, LORD (1962), *Facing the Dictators*, Cassell
AVON, LORD (1960), *Full Circle*, Cassell
BIRCH, A. (1967), *The British System of Government*, Allen & Unwin
BLAXLAND, G. (1964), *J. H. Thomas, A Life of Unity*, Muller
BLOCK, G. (1964), *A Source Book of Conservatism*, CPC
BLONDEL, J. (1963), *Voters, Parties and Leaders*, Penguin
BOYD, F. (1956), *Richard Austen Butler*, Rockliff
BRAND, C. (1965), *The British Labour Party: A Short History*, Stanford U.P.
BROAD, L. (1956), *Winston Churchill 1874-55*, Hutchinson
BROAD, L. (1964), *Winston Churchill, the Years of Achievement*, Sidgwick & Jackson
BROMHEAD, P. (1958), *The House of Lords and Contemporary Politics*, Routledge & Kegan Paul
BUTLER, D. (1963), *The Electoral System in Britain 1918-1951*, O.U.P.
BUTT, R. (1967), *The Power of Parliament*, Constable
CECIL, LADY G. (1921-32), *Life of Robert, Marquess of Salisbury*, 4 vols. Hodder & Stoughton
CHILSTON, LORD (1965), *W. H. Smith*, Routledge & Kegan Paul
CLYNES, J. (1937), *Memoirs*, 2 vols., Hutchinson
COOTE, C. (1965), *A Companion of Honour*, Collins
COWLES, VIRGINIA (1953), *Winston Churchill: the Era and the Man*, Hamish Hamilton
CREWE, LORD (1931), *Lord Rosebery*, 2 vols., Murray
CRICK, B. (1966), *The Reform of Parliament*, Weidenfeld & Nicolson

CROSSMAN, R. (1963), Introduction to Bagehot's. '*The English Constitution*', Fontana

DAHL, R. (ed) (1967), *Political Oppositions in Western Democracies*, Yale

DALTON, H. (1953), *Call Back Yesterday*, Muller

ELLIOT, A. (1911), *Life of Goschen 1831-1907*, 2 vols., Longmans

ENSOR, SIR R. (1966), *England, 1870-1914*, O.U.P.

FEILING, SIR K. (1924), *A History of the Tory Party*, O.U.P.

FEILING, SIR K. (1938), *The Second Tory Party*, Macmillan

FEILING, SIR K. (1946), *The Life of Neville Chamberlain*, Macmillan

FOOT, M. (1962), *Aneurin Bevan, 1897-1945*, MacGibbon & Kee

FULFORD, R. (1967), *Samuel Whitbread 1764-1815*, Macmillan

GOLLIN, A. (1965), *Balfour's Burden*, Blond.

HALDANE, R. (1929), *An Autobiography*, Hodder & Stoughton

HALEVY, E. (1951), *A History of the English People in the Nineteenth Century*, Vol. IV, Benn

HAMILTON, MARY (1938), *Arthur Henderson: A Biography*, Heinemann

HANSON AND WISEMAN (1962), *Parliament at Work*, Stevens

HARRISON, M. (1960), *Trade Unions and the Labour Party since 1945*, Allen & Unwin

HOBHOUSE, C. (1964), *Fox*, Murray

HOGG, Q. (1947), *The Purpose of Parliament*, Blandford Press

HOWARD AND WEST (1965), *The Making of the Prime Minister*, Cape

JENKINS, R. (1954), *Mr Balfour's Poodle*, Heinemann

JENKINS, R. (1948), *Mr Attlee*, Heinemann

JENNINGS, SIR I. (1958), *Cabinet Government*, Cambridge U.P.

JENNINGS, SIR I. (1960-62), *Party Politics*, 3 vols., Cambridge U.P.

LEONARD, R. (1964), *Guide to the General Election*, Pan

LUCY, SIR H. (1885), *A Diary of Two Parliaments*, Cassell

LUCY, SIR H. (1901), *A Diary of the Unionist Parliament*, Arrowsmith

MCNAIR, J. (1955), *James Maxton: The Beloved Rebel*, Allen & Unwin

MACNEILL WEIR, L. (1938), *The Tragedy of Ramsay MacDonald*, London

MACLEOD, I. (1961), *Neville Chamberlain*, Muller

MARSHALL AND MOODIE (1961), *Some Problems of the Constitution*, Hutchinson

MILLER, J. D. B. (1960), *Politicians*, Leicester U.P.

MINNEY, R. (1958), *Viscount Addison, Leader of the Lords*, Odhams

NAMIER, SIR L. (1961), *The Structure of Politics at the Accession of George III*, Macmillan

NORWICH, LORD (1953), *Old Men Forget*, Hart-Davies

PARES, R. (1953), *King George III and the Politicians*, O.U.P.

PELLING, H. (1965), *The Origins of the Labour Party*, O.U.P.

PELLING, H. (1965), *A Short History of the Labour Party*, Macmillan

PLUMB, J. (1956), *Sir Robert Walpole*, Cressett Press

POSTGATE, R. (1951), *Life of George Lansbury*, Longmans

RAMSAY, A. (1928), *Sir Robert Peel*, London

REID, WEMYSS (1889), *Life of Forster*, Chapman & Hall

ROBERTS, M. (1939), *The Whig Party*, London

ROSE, R. (1965), *Politics in England*, Faber

SHINWELL, E. (1955), *Conflict Without Malice*, Odhams

SOMMER, D. (1960), *Haldane of Cloan*, Allen & Unwin

SOUTHGATE, D. (1966), *The Most English Minister*, Macmillan

SPENDER, J. A. (1923), *Life of Sir Henry Campbell-Bannerman*, 2 vols., Hodder & Stoughton

SMITH, L. (1964), *Harold Wilson*, Fontana

SWINTON, LORD (1948), *I Remember*, Hutchinson

TAYLOR, A. J. P. (1965), *English History 1914-1945*, Oxford U.P.

TAYLOR, E. (1965), *The House of Commons at Work*, Pelican

THOMSON, D. (1965), *England in the Twentieth Century*, Pelican

WEBB, BEATRICE (1956), *Diaries 1924-32*, Longmans

WHEELER-BENNETT, SIR J. (1962), *John Anderson, Viscount Waverley*, Macmillan

WILDING AND LAUNDY (1968), *An Encyclopaedia of Parliament*, Cassell

WILLIAMS, B. (1943), *Carteret and Newcastle*, Cambridge U.P.

WILSON, T. (1966), *The Downfall of the Liberals 1914-1935*, Collins

WISEMAN, H. V. (1966), *Parliament and the Executive*, Routledge & Kegan Paul

YOUNG, G. M. (1952), *Stanley Baldwin*, Hart-Davis

YOUNG, K. (1963), *Arthur James Balfour*, Bell

Note on Sources

The Shadow Cabinet is a subject upon which there is remarkably little published material. There are no books written specifically about this body, what few references there are being scattered through most of the standard works on British Government. Both R. T. McKenzie's *British Political Parties* and J. P. Mackintosh's *The British Cabinet* touch upon the subject in more detail, though neither constitutes a comprehensive study. The most recent work to include material concerned with the Shadow Cabinet is that by R. K. Alderman and J. A. Cross on *The Tactics of Resignation*.

The memoirs and diaries of politicians undoubtedly throw some light upon the workings of Shadow Cabinets in the past, as do a number of the biographies of leading statesmen, but too often emphasis is placed upon the periods in office rather than those spent in Opposition. The Press and the Political Parties both provide valuable reports and records though, here again, there are any number of shortcomings. Press coverage of the activities of the Shadow Cabinet has only in recent years dealt adequately with this subject, no doubt due largely to the failure of the Political Parties to provide the Press with full information regarding the activities of the Shadow

Cabinet. For example, it appears through contact with the Labour Party headquarters at Transport House that it is policy not to publish the lists of Front Bench spokesmen; and because there are often changes during the course of a parliamentary session, no annual lists are available. Such information is thus drawn from the Press, when available, and from such works as *Kessing's Contemporary Archives* which gives details of changes at regular intervals. R. T. McKenzie's *British Political Parties* and Butler and Freeman's *British Political Facts 1900-1967*, contain lists of the P.L.P. Parliamentary Committee and Shadow Cabinet, as do the later copies of the Labour Party *Annual Conference Reports*. Conservative Party Conference Reports provide no such information and it would appear through contact with Geoffrey Block of the Conservative Research Department that comprehensive records of Conservative Shadow Cabinet membership do not exist.

The weekly press, with the possible exception of *The Economist*, rarely contains any information regarding the Shadow Cabinet which is of more than general interest, whilst the academic quarterlies are also, surprisingly, lacking in this respect. However, a new journal called *Government and Opposition* has recently appeared which might do something to correct this imbalance between the study of Government and Opposition. The *Hansard* reports of parliamentary debates provide an invaluable and readily accessible fund of information concerning both the membership and procedure of 'Her Majesty's Opposition', though references to the 'Shadow Cabinet', as such, are unknown. Television, on the other hand, has in recent years provided an excellent 'pictorial' supplement to the existing channels of political communication, members of the viewing public being given the opportunity to 'meet' those who constitute both the Cabinet and the Shadow Cabinet.